Contents

Vintage Knits
for Him & Her

30 modern knitting patterns
for stylish vintage knitwear

D&C
David and Charles

www.stitchcraftcreate.co.uk

The '50s

"Mad Men" flair and "New Look" style for a feminine
shape that's chic and glamorous

1
Shawl collar jacket

A cable and rib jacket with shawl collar. Aran weight yarn such as Phil Harmony.

2
Short-sleeved sweater

Striking Fair Isle top with ribbed edging.
Sport weight yarn such as Partner 3.5.

1 Shawl collar jacket

SIZES
S (15-17 yrs), M (42-44), L (46-48), XL (50-52), XXL (54-56)
(see Sizing Charts)
S (M, L, XL, XXL)

MATERIALS
Aran weight yarn such as Phil Harmony from Phildar (51% wool and 49% acrylic): **16 (17, 19, 20, 22)** balls, colour shown here is Grenat • Pair each 4.5mm and 5mm needles • Cable needle • 6 Buttons

STITCHES USED
K1, P1 rib and K3, P3 rib
Cable pattern stitch: see charts and legends

TENSION
It is essential to check your tension before starting your garment to ensure you get the right measurements.
On 5mm needles, 38 sts and 49 rows to 20cm in pattern stitch.

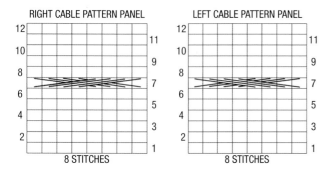

RIGHT CABLE PATTERN PANEL   LEFT CABLE PATTERN PANEL

8 STITCHES   8 STITCHES

K on RS; P on WS.

C8F: slip next 4 sts onto cable needle and leave at front of work, K4 then K4 from cable needle.

C8B: slip next 4 sts onto cable needle and leave at back of work, K4 then K4 from cable needle.

INSTRUCTIONS
BACK
With 4.5mm needles, cast on **95 (99, 103, 115, 121)** sts and work 7cm in K1, P1 rib. Change to 5mm needles and cont in patt, as follows:
S: *P3, K3, P3, right cable patt panel 8 sts (see chart), P3, K3*, rep from * to * twice then °P3, K3, P3, left cable patt panel 8 sts (see chart), P3, K3,° rep from ° to ° twice ending with P3.
M: K2, *P3, K3, P3, right cable patt panel 8 sts (see chart), P3, K3*, rep from * to * twice then °P3, K3, P3, left cable patt panel 8 sts (see chart), P3, K3°, rep from ° to ° twice, ending with P3 and K2.
L: K4, *P3, K3, P3, right cable patt panel 8 sts (see chart), P3, K3*, rep from * to * twice then °P3, K3, P3, left cable patt panel 8 sts (see chart), P3, K3 °, rep from ° to ° twice, ending with P3 and K4.
XL: K4, P3, K3, * P3, K3, P3, right cable patt panel 8 sts (see chart), P3, K3 *, rep from * to * twice then °P3, K3, P3, left cable patt panel 8 sts (see chart), P3, K3°, rep from ° to ° twice ending with P3, K3, P3 and K4.
XXL: P4, K3, P3, K3, * P3, K3, P3, right cable patt panel 8 sts (see chart), P3, K3*, rep from * to * twice then °P3, K3, P3, left cable patt panel 8 sts (see chart), P3, K3°, rep from ° to ° twice ending with P3, K3, P3, K3 and P4.
Cont in patt as set until work measures 39cm from end of ribbing, then shape armholes by casting off at beg of each row as follows:
Armhole Rows 1, 2: Cast off **4 (4, 4, 4, 4)** sts, patt to end
Rows 3, 4: Cast off **3 (3, 3, 3, 3)** sts, patt to end
Rows 5, 6: Cast off **2 (2, 2, 3, 3)** sts, patt to end
Rows 7, 8: Cast off **2 (2, 2, 2, 2)** sts, patt to end
Rows 9, 10: Cast off **1 (1, 1, 2, 2)** st, patt to end
Rows 11, 12, 13, 14: Cast off **0 (0, 0, 1, 1)**, patt to end.
71 (75, 79, 83, 89) sts remain.
When work measures **59 (60, 61, 62, 63)** cm from end of ribbing, shape shoulders and neck as follows:
Shoulder row 1: Cast off **6 (6,7,7,8)** sts, patt 23 sts, cast off **13 (15, 15, 17, 17)** sts, patt to end
Row 2: Cast off **6 (6, 7, 7, 8)** sts, patt to neck edge (**23 sts**). Turn
Row 3: Cast off 11 sts at neck edge, then patt to end **(12 sts)**
Row 4: Cast off **6 (6, 7, 7, 8)** sts, patt to neck edge **(6 sts)**
Row 5: Patt
Row 6: Cast off remaining **6 (7,7,8,9)** sts
Join yarn to other side of neck and complete, reversing shapings (from Row 3).

RIGHT FRONT

With 4.5mm needles, cast on **45 (47, 51, 55, 59)** sts and work 7cm in K1, P1 rib.
Change to 5mm needles, inc **1 (1,0,1,0)** st on first row and work in patt as follows:

S: K3, P3, left cable patt panel 8 sts (see chart), P3, K3, P3, K3, P3, left cable patt panel 8 sts (see chart), P3, K3, P3.

M: K3, P3, left cable patt panel 8 sts (see chart), P3, K3, P3, K3, P3, left cable patt panel 8 sts (see chart), P3, K3, P3, K2.

L: K4, P3, left cable patt panel 8 sts (see chart), P3, K3, P3, K3, P3, left cable patt panel 8 sts (see chart), P3, K3, P3, K4.

XL: K3, P3, left cable patt panel 8 sts (see chart), P3, K3, P3, K3, P3, left cable panel patt 8 sts (see chart), P3, K3, P3, K3, P3, K4.

XXL: K3, P3, K3, P3, left cable patt panel 8 sts (see chart), P3, K3, P3, K3, P3, left cable patt panel 8 sts (see chart), P3, K3, P3, K3 and P4.

46 (48, 51, 56, 59) sts.

Continue in pattern until work measures **32 (33, 34, 35, 36)** cm from end of rib.
Shape front slope by casting off 1 st at RH (front) edge on next row and rep as follows:

S: every 4th row, 12 times and every 6th row, 3 times

M: every 4th row, 15 times and then on the following 6th row once

L: On following alt row once and then every 4th row, 16 times

XL: On following alt row once and then every 4th row, 16 times

XXL: On following alt row once and then every 4th row, 16 times.

When work measures 39cm from end of ribbing, shape armhole by casting off at LH (armhole) edge every alt row as follows:

Armhole row 1: Cast off **4 (4, 4, 4, 4)** sts, patt to end

Row 2: Patt

Row 3: Cast off **3 (3, 3, 3, 3)** sts, patt to end

Row 4: Patt

Row 5: Cast off **2 (2, 2, 3, 3)** sts, patt to end

Row 6: Patt

Row 7: Cast off **2 (2, 2, 2, 2)** sts, patt to end

Row 8: Patt

Row 9: Cast off **1 (1, 1, 2, 2)** sts, patt to end

Row 10: Patt

Row 11: Cast off **0 (0, 0, 1, 1)** sts, patt to end

Row 12: Patt

Row 13: Cast off **0 (0, 0, 1, 1)** sts, patt to end

When work measures **59 (60, 61, 62, 63)** cm from end of ribbing, shape shoulder by casting off at LH edge on every alt row as follows:

Cast off **6 (6, 7, 7, 8)** sts, patt to end

Patt

6 (6, 7, 7, 8) sts, patt to end

Patt

6 (7, 7, 8, 9) sts, patt to end

LEFT FRONT

Knit left front to match, reversing shapings and working patt panel for a right cable.

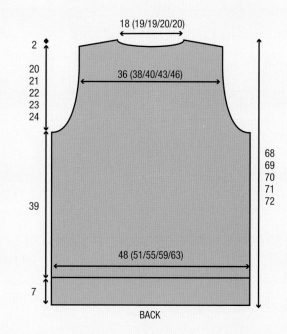

18 (19/19/20/20)

36 (38/40/43/46)

2
20
21
22
23
24

39

7

68
69
70
71
72

48 (51/55/59/63)

BACK

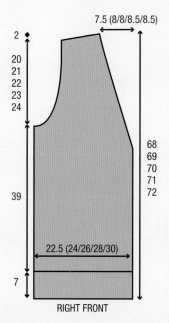

7.5 (8/8/8.5/8.5)

2
20
21
22
23
24

39

7

68
69
70
71
72

22.5 (24/26/28/30)

RIGHT FRONT

Shawl collar jacket cont'd

SLEEVES

With 4.5mm needles, cast on **48 (50, 54, 58, 62)** sts and work 7cm in K1, P1 rib.
Change to 5mm needles.Inc 1 on next row and work in patt as follows:
S: P3, K3, P3, right cable patt panel 8 sts (see chart), P3, K3, P3, K3, P3, left cable patt panel 8 sts (see chart), P3, K3, P3.
M: K1, P3, K3, P3, right cable patt panel 8 sts (see chart), P3, K3, P3, K3, P3, left cable patt panel 8 sts (see chart), P3, K3, P3 and K1.
L: K3, P3, K3, P3, right cable patt panel 8 sts (see chart), P3, K3, P3, K3, P3, left cable patt panel 8 sts (see chart), P3, K3, P3 and K3.
XL: P2, K3, P3, K3, P3, right cable patt panel 8 sts (see chart), P3, K3, P3, K3, P3, left cable patt panel 8 sts (see chart), P3, K3, P3, K3 and P2.
XXL: K1, P3, K3, P3, K3, P3, right cable patt panel 8 sts (see chart), P3, K3, P3, K3, P3, left cable patt panel 8 sts (see chart), P3, K3, P3, K3, P3 and K1.
49 (51, 55, 59, 63) sts.
Inc by 1 st each end of row as follows:
S: every 10th row twice and every 8th row, 9 times
M: every 8th row, 11 times and foll 6th row once
L: every 8th row, 11 times and foll 6th row once
XL: every 10th row, twice and every 8th row, 9 times
XXL: every 10th row, twice and every 8th row, 9 times
71 (75, 79, 81, 85) sts.
When work measures 41cm from end of ribbing, shape by casting off at beg of each row as follows:
S: 2 sts 10 times, 1 st 18 times and 2 sts 8 times
M: 3 sts twice, 2 sts 8 times, 1 st 16 times and 2 sts 10 times
L: 3 sts twice, 2 sts 10 times, 1 st 14 times, 2 sts 8 times and 3 sts twice
XL: 3 sts twice, 2 sts 10 times, 1 st 12 times, 2 sts 10 times and 3 sts twice
XXL: 3 sts 4 times, 2 sts 8 times, 1 st 12 times, 2 sts 8 times and 3 sts 4 times.
When work measures 56cm from end of ribbing then loosely cast off rem 17 sts.
Knit second sleeve to match.

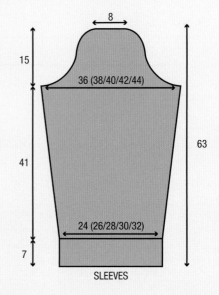

SLEEVES

SHAWL COLLAR

With 4.5mm needles, cast on **169 (173, 175, 179, 181)** sts and work in K1, P1 rib, starting first row and every odd row (RS) with K2.
When work measures 3cm start shaping the collar.
Next row: Leave **75 (77, 79, 81, 83)** sts from right side (i.e. K2 end) on a stitch holder and rib to end.
Next row: Rib
Next three alternate rows: Leave 5 sts from K2 end on holder and continue in rib patt.
Next 10 alternate rows: Leave 6 sts on holder and patt in rib to end
Work one row rib across all sts then work a few rows of st st in another yarn in a different colour.

Press these rows, they will be unpicked when attaching the collar to the jacket.
Knit a second piece, reversing all shaping and make 6 buttonholes over 2 sts, positioning first buttonhole **4 (5, 3, 3, 3)** sts from edge and the rest spaced **11 (11, 12, 13, 13)** sts apart.

POCKET

With 5mm needles, cast on 15 sts and work in K3, P3 rib, starting and ending first row and every odd row (RS) with P3.
When work measures 9cm, change to 4.5mm needles and work in K1, P1 rib, starting and ending first row and every odd row (RS) with K2.
Cont until work measures 11cm then loosely cast off in rib.

TO MAKE UP AND FINISH

Join shoulder, side and sleeve seams. Sew sleeves into armholes. Graft wide ends of collar together then attach collar to front edges and neck, st by st, using back stitch on RS of work. Sew pocket to left front, **39 (40, 41, 42, 43)** cm up from bottom. Sew on buttons.

2 Short-sleeved sweater

SIZES
34-36 (38-40, 42-44, 46-48, 50-52) (see Sizing Charts)

MATERIALS
5-ply or Sport weight yarn such as Partner 3.5 from Phildar (50% polyamide, 25% worsted wool and 25% acrylic): 5 (5, 6, 6, 7) balls of main colour (M), shown here in Aviateur shade; 2 (2, 2, 2, 2) balls of contrast colour (A), shown in Écru • Pair each 3mm and 3.5mm needles

STITCHES USED
K1, P1 rib
Stocking stitch
Fair Isle pattern (stranded knitting worked in st st): see chart and legends

TENSION
It is essential to check your tension before starting your garment to ensure you get the right measurements.
On 3.5mm needles, 24 sts and 30 rows to 10cm in st st.
On 3.5mm needles, 24 sts and 30 rows to 10cm in Fair Isle patt. worked in st st

INSTRUCTIONS:
BACK
With 3mm needles, cast on 106 (112, 122, 132, 146) sts using M and work 2cm in K1, P1 rib.
Change to 3.5mm needles and cont in st st, using M. Dec 1 in the 3rd st from each end of row, as follows:
every 6th row 8 (0, 0, 0, 0) times, every 8th row 0 (6, 6, 2, 6) times, every

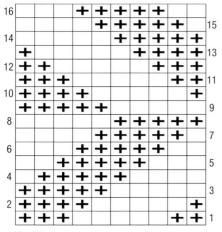

10 stitches
Repeat the 10 sts and 16 rows shown in chart

   Main colour (M)
+ Contrast colour (A)

10th row 0 (0, 0, 3, 0) times. 90 (100, 110, 122, 134) sts remain.
When work measures 18cm from end of ribbing, inc 1 in 3rd stitch from each end of next row, then rep as follows:
34-36: Every 12th row, twice and every 10th row, twice
38-40, 42-44, 50-52: Every 14th row, 3 times
46-48: foll 28th row once 100 (108, 118, 126, 142) sts.
When work measures 36cm from end of ribbing, shape armholes by casting off at beg of each row as follows:
34-36, 38-40: 4 sts twice, 3 sts twice, 2 sts twice and 1 st 4 times
42-44: 4 sts twice, 3 sts 4 times, 2 sts 4 times and 1 st 6 times
46-48: 5 sts twice, 4 sts twice, 3 sts 4 times, 2 sts 4 times and 1 st twice
50-52: 5 sts twice, 4 sts 4 times, 3 sts 4 times, 2 sts 4 times and 1 st 6 times
78 (82, 84, 86, 90) sts remain.
When work measures 55 (56, 57, 58, 59) cm from end of ribbing, shape shoulders by casting off at beg of every alt row at outside edge as follows:
34-36: 5 sts 3 times
38-40: 5 sts once and 6 sts twice
42-44, 46-48: 6 sts 3 times
50-52: 6 sts once and 7 sts twice
At the same time, shape neck by casting off the centre 16 (16, 16, 18, 18) sts then cont, working one side at a time, casting off 8 sts at neck edge every alt row, twice. Repeat to match on other side of neck.

FRONT
With 3mm needles, cast on 106 (112, 122, 132, 146) sts using M and work 2cm in K1, P1 rib.
Change to 3.5mm needles, cont in st st, following Fair Isle patt on chart, and dec 1 in 3rd st from each end of row as follows:
34-36: every 6th row, 8 times
38-40, 42-44, 50-52: every 8th row, 6 times
46-68: every 10th row, 3 times and every 8th row, twice. 90 (100, 110, 122, 134) sts remain.
When work measures 18cm from end of ribbing, inc 1st in 3rd stitch from each end of next row and then rep as follows:
34-36: every 12th row twice and every 10th row twice
38-40, 42-44, 50-52: every 14th row, 3 times
46-48: on foll 28th row once. 100 (108, 118, 126, 142) sts remain.
When work measures 36cm from end of ribbing, shape armholes by casting off at beg of each row as follows:
34-36: 4 sts twice, 3 sts twice, 2 sts twice and 1 st 4 times
38-40: 4 sts twice, 3 sts twice, 2 sts 4 times and 1 st 4 times
42-44: 4 sts twice, 3 sts 4 times, 2 sts 4 times and 1 st 6 times
46-48: 5 sts twice, 4 sts twice, 3 sts 4 times, 2 sts 4 times and 1 st twice
50-52: 5 sts twice, 4 sts 4 times, 3 sts 4 times, 2 sts 4 times and 1 st 6 times
78 (82, 84, 86, 90) sts remain.
When work measures 47 (48, 49, 50, 51) cm from end of ribbing, shape neck by

casting off the centre **14 (14, 14, 16, 16)** sts then cont, working one side at a time and cast off at neck edge on every alt row as follows: 4 sts once, 3 sts once, 2 sts twice, 1 st 3 times and then cast off 1 st on every following 4th row 3 times. When work measures **55 (56, 57, 58, 59)** cm from end of ribbing, shape shoulder by casting off at armhole edge on every alt row as follows:
34-36: 5 sts 3 times
38-40: 5 sts once and 6 sts twice
42-44, 46-48: 6 sts 3 times
50-52: 6 sts once and 7 sts twice
Repeat on other side of neck.

SLEEVES

With 3mm needles, cast on **74 (78, 84, 88, 94)** sts using M and work 2cm in K1, P1 rib. Change to 3.5mm needles and cont in st st, using M.
When work measures 3cm from end of ribbing, shape by casting off at beg of each row as follows:
34-36: 2 sts 8 times, 1st 14 times, work 2 rows straight then 1st 16 times and 2 sts 6 times
38-40: 2 sts 10 times, 1 st 12 times, work 2 rows

straight then 1 st 14 times and 2 sts 8 times
42-44: 3 sts twice, 2 sts 8 times, 1 st 12 times, work 2 rows straight then 1 st 12 times then 2 sts 8 times and 3 sts twice
46-48: 3 sts twice, 2 sts 10 times, 1 st 10 times, work 2 rows straight then 1 st 10 times, 2 sts 10 times and 3 sts twice
50-52: 3 sts 4 times, 2 sts 10 times, 1 st 8 times, work 2 rows straight then 1 st 10 times, 2 sts 8 times and 3 sts 4 times
When work measures 18cm from end of ribbing, loosely cast off rem 16 sts.
Knit second sleeve in same way.

NECKBAND

With 3mm needles, cast on **146 (146, 146, 150, 150)** sts using M and work 2cm in K1, P1 rib then do a K row on RS and a few rows of st st in another shade.
Press these rows, they will be unpicked when assembling the sweater.

TO MAKE UP AND FINISH

Join shoulder, side and sleeve seams. Sew sleeves into armholes. Sew on neckband, st by st, using back st, on RS of work.

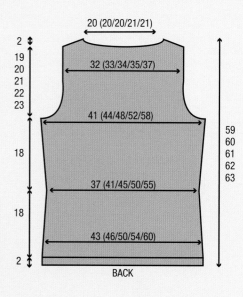

20 (20/20/21/21)

2
19
20
21
22
23

32 (33/34/35/37)

41 (44/48/52/58)

18

37 (41/45/50/55)

18

43 (46/50/54/60)

2

59
60
61
62
63

BACK

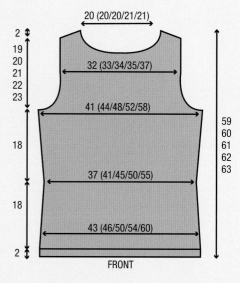

20 (20/20/21/21)

2
19
20
21
22
23

32 (33/34/35/37)

41 (44/48/52/58)

18

37 (41/45/50/55)

18

43 (46/50/54/60)

2

59
60
61
62
63

FRONT

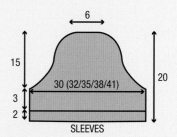

6

15

30 (32/35/38/41)

20

3
2

SLEEVES

3
³/₄ Sleeve sweater

Decorative pattern stitch and
K2, P2 rib.
Aran weight yarn, such as Phildar
Laine, Mohair & Soie.

4
Belted gilet

Stocking stitch with
garter stitch edging.
Aran weight such as
Phil Ourson.

3 ³/₄ Sleeve sweater

SIZES

34-36 (38-40, 42-44, 46-48, 50-52) (see Sizing Charts)

MATERIALS

Aran weight yarn such as Phildar's Laine, Mohair & Soie (50% mohair, 30% silk and 20% wool): 12 (13, 14, 15, 17) balls, shown here in Anthracite shade • Pair of 3.5mm needles • French knitting bobbin

STITCHES USED

K2, P2 rib
Decorative pattern stitch: see chart and legends
NB. only do YO if compensated for by PSSO and vice versa.

TENSION

It is essential to check your tension before starting your garment to ensure you get the right measurements.
On 3.5mm needles, 51 sts and 55 rows to 20cm working in patt
On 3.5mm needles, 51 sts and 52 rows to 20cm in K2, P2 rib

INSTRUCTIONS

BACK

With 3.5mm needles, cast on **114 (122, 134, 142, 162)** sts and work 12cm in K2, P2 rib, starting and ending first row and every odd row (RS) with K2.
Still using 3.5mm needles, work in patt as shown in chart, dec 1 (inc 1, dec 1, inc 1, inc 1) on first row and starting with 1 edge st and first st on chart.
113 (123, 133, 143, 163) sts.
Dec 1 st at each end of row as follows:
34-36, 38-40, 42-44: every 4th row 5 times
46-48: every 6th row 3 times
50-52: every 4th row 3 times and every alt row 4 times **103 (113, 123, 137, 149)** sts remain.
When work measures 8cm from end of ribbing, inc 1 st each end of foll row and then rep as follows:
34-36, 38-40: every 12th row 3 times and foll 10th row once
42-44: every 12th row, 3 times and foll 10th row, once
46-48: foll 20th row once and foll 18th row once
50-52: every 8th row, 6 times. **113 (123, 133, 143, 163)** sts.

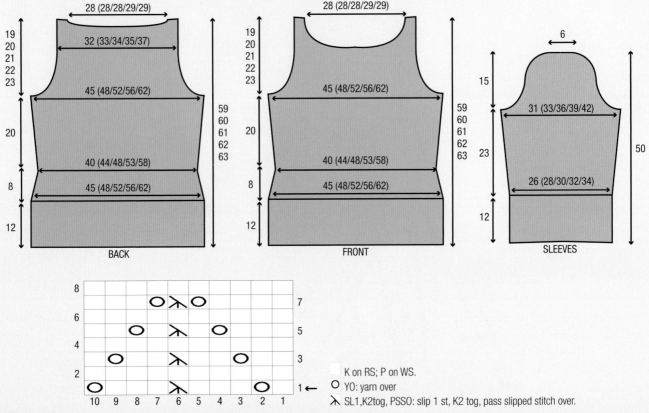

BACK

FRONT

SLEEVES

K on RS; P on WS.
O YO: yarn over
⋏ SL1,K2tog, PSSO: slip 1 st, K2 tog, pass slipped stitch over.

When work measures 28cm from end of ribbing, shape armholes by casting off at beg of each row as follows:

34-36: 4 sts twice, 3 sts 4 times, 2 sts 4 times and 1 st twice

38-40: 5 sts twice, 4 sts twice, 3 sts 4 times, 2 sts 4 times and 1 st twice

42-44: 5 sts twice, 4 sts twice, 3 sts 4 times, 2 sts 6 times and 1 st twice

46-48: 5 sts twice, 4 sts 4 times, 3 sts 4 times, 2 sts 4 times and 1 st 4 times

50-52: 6 sts twice, 5 sts twice, 4 sts 4 times, 3 sts 4 times, 2 sts 6 times and 1 st 4 times. **83 (83, 89, 93, 97)** sts remain.

When work measures **45 (46, 47, 48, 49)** cm from end of ribbing, shape neck by casting off the centre **31 (31, 31, 33, 33)** sts then cont to work one side at a time and cast off 10 sts at neck edge every alt row, twice.

When work measures **47 (48, 49, 50, 51)** cm from end of ribbing, cast off rem **6 (6, 9, 10, 12)** sts for shoulder. Finish other side of neck.

FRONT

With 3.5mm needles, cast on **114 (122, 134, 142, 162)** sts and work 12cm in K2, P2 rib, starting and ending first row and every odd row (RS) with K2. Still using 3.5mm needles, cont in patt as set in chart, and dec 1 (inc 1, dec 1, inc 1, inc 1) st on first row, starting with 1 edge st and first st on chart.

113 (123, 133, 143, 163) sts.

Dec 1 st at each end of row as follows:

34-36, 38-40, 42-44: every 4th row 5 times

46-48: every 6th row 3 times

50-52: every 4th row, 3 times and every alt row, 4 times. **103 (113, 123, 137, 149)** sts remain.

When work measures 8cm from end of ribbing, inc 1 st each end of foll row and then repeat as follows:

34-36, 38-40, 42-44: every 12th row 3 times and foll 10th row once

46-48: foll 20th row once and foll 18th row once

50-52: every 8th row 6 times. **113 (123, 133, 143, 163)** sts.

When work measures 28cm from end of ribbing, shape armholes by casting off at beg of each row as follows:

34-36: 4 sts twice, 3 sts 4 times, 2 sts 4 times and 1 st twice

38-40: 5 sts twice, 4 sts twice, 3 sts 4 times, 2 sts 4 times and 1 st twice

42-44: 5 sts twice, 4 sts twice, 3 sts 4 times, 2 sts

6 times and 1 st twice

46-48: 5 sts twice, 4 sts 4 times, 3 sts 4 times, 2 sts 4 times and 1 st 4 times

50-52: 6 sts twice, 5 sts twice, 4 sts 4 times, 3 sts 4 times, 2 sts 6 times and 1 st 4 times. **83 (83, 89, 93, 97)** sts remain.

When work measures **39 (40, 41, 42, 43)** cm from end of ribbing, shape neck by casting off the centre **25 (25, 25, 27, 27)** sts then cont to work one side at a time and dec at neck edge every alt row: 5 sts once, 4 sts twice, 3 sts once, 2 sts once and 1 st 5 times.

When work measures **47 (48, 49, 50, 51)** cm from end of ribbing, cast off rem **6 (6, 9, 10, 12)** sts for shoulder. Finish other side of neck.

SLEEVES

With 3.5mm needles, cast on **66 (74, 78, 82, 90)** sts and work 12cm in K2, P2 rib, starting and ending first row and every odd row (RS) with K2. Still using 3.5mm needles, work in patt from chart. Inc 1 (dec 1, inc 1, inc 1, dec 1) on first row and start with: 8th st on chart (1 edge st and first st on chart, 2nd st on chart, 1 edge st and first st on chart, 2nd st on chart).

67 (73, 79, 83, 89) sts.

Inc 1 st each end, incorporating sts into patt as follows:

34-36: every 8th row 5 times and every 6th row 3 times

38-40, 42-44: every 8th row 7 times

46-48, 50-52: every 6th row 10 times. **83 (87, 93, 103, 109)** sts remain.

When work measures 23cm from end of ribbing, shape by casting off at beg of each row as follows:

34-36: 3 sts twice, 2 sts 8 times, 1 st 22 times, 2 sts 8 times and 3 sts twice

38-40: 3 sts twice, 2 sts 10 times, 1 st 18 times, 2 sts 10 times and 3 sts twice

42-44: 3 sts 4 times, 2 sts 10 times, 1 st 14 times, 2 sts 12 times and 3 sts twice

46-48: 3 sts 4 times, 2 sts 14 times, 1 st 6 times, 2 sts 14 times and 3 sts 4 times

50-52: 3 sts 6 times, 2 sts 14 times, 1 st 4 times, 2 sts 12 times and 3 sts 6 times.

17 sts remain on all sizes.

When work measures 38cm from end of ribbing, loosely cast off rem 17 sts.

Knit second sleeve in same way.

COLLAR

With 3.5mm needles, cast on **130 (130, 130, 134, 134)** sts and work in K2, P2 rib, starting and ending first row and every odd row (RS) with K2. Dec 1 st at each end of every 4th row, 16 times. **98 (98, 98, 102, 102)** sts remain.

When work measures 25cm, do a K row on RS and a few rows of st st in another shade. Press these rows, they will be unpicked when sewing on the collar. Do a second piece in same way.

TO MAKE UP AND FINISH

Join shoulder, side and sleeve seams. Sew sleeves into armholes. Join 2 collar pieces tog and sew in place around neckline with collar seams on RS of work at shoulders (seams are under collar when collar is folded down). Make a strip of French knitting, about 95cm long, thread it between collar rows on LH side, pull tight and fasten (see photo).

4 *Belted gilet*

SIZES
34-36 (38-40, 42-44, 46-48, 50-52) (see Sizing Charts)

MATERIALS
Any Aran weight yarn such as Phil Ourson from Phildar (88% acrylic and
12% polyamide): **6 (7, 8, 8, 9)** balls, shown here in Châtaigne shade • Pair of
3.5mm needles • 1 belt buckle • 1 press stud, 18mm in diameter

STITCHES USED
Garter stitch
Stocking stitch

TENSION
It is essential to check your tension before starting your garment to ensure you
get the right measurements.
On 3.5mm needles, 17 sts and 34 rows to 10cm in st st.

INSTRUCTIONS
BACK
With 3.5mm needles, cast on **72 (76, 84, 90, 100)** sts and working in st st, dec
1 in 3rd st from each end of row as follows:
34-36 and 42-44: every 16 rows, 3 times
38-40, 46-48, 50-52: foll 22nd row, once and foll 20th row, once. **66 (72, 78,
86, 96)** sts remain.
When work measures 17cm in total, form 2 belt loops as follows: leave **12 (15,
18, 22, 27)** end sts on holder and work 2cm on the next 4 sts, then leave those
4 sts on holder at front of work. Do same at other end of row for 2nd loop.
Continuing in st st, work the **12 (15, 18, 22, 27)** sts from the holder, pick up 4
sts on WS of first loop at the base of the 2cm piece you knitted, work the 34
central sts, pick up 4 sts at the base of the WS of second loop and work the
final **12 (15, 18, 22, 27)** sts.
Cont in st st until work measures 19cm in total. Now work **13 (16, 19, 23, 28)**
sts in st st, *insert RHN into first st of loop on holder and into next st on LHN
and K2tog*, rep from * to * 4 times in tot, work next 34 sts, *insert RHN into
first st of loop on holder and into next st on LHN and K2tog*, rep from * to * 4
times in tot then work final **13 (16, 19, 23, 28)** sts.
Meanwhile, when work measures 18cm, inc 1 st each end of row and then
rep as follows:
34-36, 42-44: every 20th row, twice
38-40, 46-48, 50-52: foll 30th row, once. **72 (76, 84, 90, 100)** sts.
When work measures 35cm, shape capped sleeves by inc 1 st each end of
next row and then rep as follows: every 4th row, 9 times (every 4th row, 10
times, every 6th row, 4 times and every 4th row, 5 times,every 6th row, 6 times
and every 4th row, 3 times, every 6th row, 5 times and every 4th row, 5 times).
92 (98, 104, 110, 122) sts.
When work measures **47 (48, 49, 50, 51)** cm, shape shoulders by casting off
at beg of each row as follows:
34-36: 1 st 18 times and 2 sts 22
38-40: 1 st 12 times and 2 sts 28 times
42-44: 1 st 6 times and 2 sts 34 times
46-48: 1 st twice and 2 sts 38 times
50-52: 2 sts 30 times and 3 sts 10 times.
When work measures **58 (59, 60, 61, 62)** cm, cast off rem **30 (30, 30, 32,
32)** sts.

RIGHT FRONT

With 3.5mm needles, cast on **44 (46, 50, 53, 58)** sts, work in st st, and dec 1 in 3rd st from LH edge as follows:

34-36, 42-44: every 16 rows, 3 times

38-40, 46-48, 50-52: once on the following 22nd row and once on foll 20th row

41 (44, 47, 51, 56) sts remain.

When work measures 17cm in total, form 1 belt loop as follows: leave 25 RH sts on holder and work 2cm on next 4 sts, then leave those 4 sts on holder at front of work.

Work the 25 sts from the holder in st st, then pick up 4 sts at the base of WS of loop, then work the final **12 (15, 18, 22, 27)** sts.

Cont in st st until work measures 19cm. Work 25 sts in st st, *insert RHN into first st on holder and into next st on LHN and K2tog*, rep from * to * 4 times in tot, then work final **13 (16, 19, 23, 28)** sts.

Meanwhile, when work measures 18cm in tot, inc 1 st at LH edge then rep as follows: every 20th row, twice (foll 30th row, once, every 20th row, twice, foll 30th row, once, foll 30th row once). **44 (46, 50, 53, 58)** sts.

When work measures 35cm in tot, shape capped sleeve by inc 1 st at LH edge and then rep as follows: every 4th row, 9 times (every 4th row 10 times; every 6th row 4 times and every 4th row 5 times; every 6th row 6 times and every 4th row, 3 times; every 6th row 5 times and every 4th row 5 times).

At the same time, shape neck by casting off 1 st at RH edge and then rep as follows:

34-36, 38-40, 42-44: every 8th row 9 times and every 10th row 3 times

46-48, 50-52: every 8th row 13 times.

When work measures **47 (48, 49, 50, 51)** cm, shape shoulder by casting off at LH edge every alt row as follows:

34-36: 1 st 9 times and 2 sts 11 times

38-40: 1 st 6 times and 2 sts 14 times

42-44: 1 st 3 times and 2 sts 17 times

46-48: 1 st once and 2 sts 19 times

50-52: 2 sts 15 times and 3 sts 5 times.

When work measures **67 (68, 69, 70.5, 71.5)** cm, cast off rem 10 sts.

Make left front as right, reversing all shaping.

BELT

With 3.5mm needles, cast on **179 (185, 191, 197, 207)** sts. Work 6 rows in garter st then cast off loosely.

TO MAKE UP AND FINISH

Join shoulder and side seams. Join collar by sewing the 10 cast off stitches of the front pieces together, and sew collar to back neckline. Fold 2cm of belt over buckle and attach with concealed stitching. Slip belt through loops.

Sew press stud onto left front edge, 18cm from bottom.

Sew second part of press stud on right front, 18cm up from bottom and 5cm in from front edge.

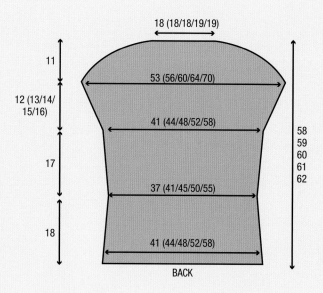

18 (18/18/19/19)

11

12 (13/14/15/16)

17

18

53 (56/60/64/70)

41 (44/48/52/58)

37 (41/45/50/55)

41 (44/48/52/58)

58
59
60
61
62

BACK

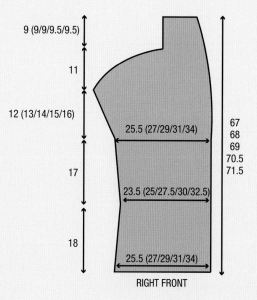

9 (9/9/9.5/9.5)

11

12 (13/14/15/16)

17

18

25.5 (27/29/31/34)

23.5 (25/27.5/30/32.5)

25.5 (27/29/31/34)

67
68
69
70.5
71.5

RIGHT FRONT

5
Sleeveless wrap around top

Stocking stitch, pattern
stitch and K1, P1 rib.
Double knitting such as Zéphir.

6
Jacket

Cable pattern and stocking stitch.
Double knitting such as Zéphir with
Chunky such as Neige.

5 Sleeveless wrap around top

SIZES
34-36 (38-40, 42-44, 46-48, 50-52) (see Sizing Charts)

MATERIALS
Double knitting such as Zéphir from Phildar (36% wool, 36% acrylic and 28% polyamide): **5 (5, 6, 7, 7)** balls, shown here in Fauve shade • Pair each 3mm and 3.5mm needles

STITCHES USED
K1, P1 rib
Stocking stitch
Pattern stitch: see chart and legends
Patterned double decrease (patt dbl dec) at 4th st from ends of row:
At RH side: K3, place next 2 sts on CN, leave at back of work, knit tog next st on LHN with first st on CN then next st on LHN tog with last st on CN.
At LH side: work to last 7 sts, place 2 sts on CN, leave at front of work, knit tog first st on CN and next st on LHN then knit tog last st on CN with next st on LHN then K3.
Single st decrease (sgl st dec) at 4th st from ends of row:
At RH side: K3, K2tog
At LH side: work to last 5 sts then SL1, K1, PSSO (Slip 1 knitwise, K1, pass slipped stitch over), K3

TENSION
It is essential to check your tension before starting your garment to ensure you get the right measurements.
On 3.5mm needles, 20 sts and 33 rows to 10cm in st st
On 3.5mm needles, 41 sts and 71 rows to 20cm in pattern stitch

INSTRUCTIONS
BACK
With 3mm needles, cast on **83 (89, 97, 105, 117)** sts and work 7cm in K1, P1 rib.
Change to 3.5mm needles and cont in st st, inc 1 st in middle or end of first row. **84 (90, 98, 106, 118)** sts.
Inc 1st in 3rd st from each end of row as follows: on foll 30th row, once and foll 28th row, once. **88 (94, 102, 110, 122)** sts.
When work measures 26cm from end of ribbing, shape raglan by casting off 2 sts each side, then dec at 4th st from ends of row as follows:
34-36: every 4th row *1 patt dbl dec 3 times, 1 sgl st dec once*, rep from * to * 4 times in tot (losing 60 sts to leave 28).
38-40: 1 patt dbl dec every 4th row, 14 times and 1 sgl st dec 3 times (losing 66 sts to leave 28)
42-44: 1 patt dbl dec every 4th row, 17 times and 1 sgl st dec on foll alt row, once (losing 74 sts to leave 28)
46-48: 1 patt dbl dec every 4th row, 9 times, 1 patt dbl dec on foll alt row once and 1 patt dbl dec every 4th row, 9 times (losing 80 sts to leave 30)
50-52: Work (1 patt dbl dec every 4th row, 3 times and 1 patt dbl dec on foll alt row once) 5 times, then work 1 patt dbl dec every 4th row, twice (losing 92 sts to leave 30).
When work measures **46 (47, 48, 49, 50)** cm from end of ribbing, cast off rem **28 (28, 28, 30, 30)** sts loosely.

RIGHT FRONT
With 3mm needles, cast on **83 (85, 89, 93, 99)** sts and work 7cm in K1, P1 rib, starting first row and every odd row (RS) with K2.
Change to 3.5mm needles and cont in st st, inc 1 st in middle or end of first row.
84 (86, 90, 94, 100) sts.
Inc 1 in 3rd stitch from LH edge: on foll 30th row once and on foll 28th row once.
At the same time, when work measures **0 (1, 2, 3, 4)** cm from end of ribbing, shape front edge by doing 1 patt dbl dec at 4th st from RH edge once and then as follows:
34-36: every 4th row, 1 patt dbl dec 23 times and 1 sgl st dec 11 times
38-40: every 4th row, 1 patt dbl dec 20 times and 1 sgl st dec 14 times
42-44: every 4th row, 1 patt dbl dec 22 times and 1 sgl st dec 12 times
46-48: every 4th row, 1 patt dbl dec 24 times and 1 sgl st dec 10 times

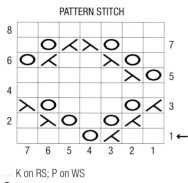

PATTERN STITCH

___ K on RS; P on WS
O YRN
X K2tog
⋋ SL1, K1, PSSO.

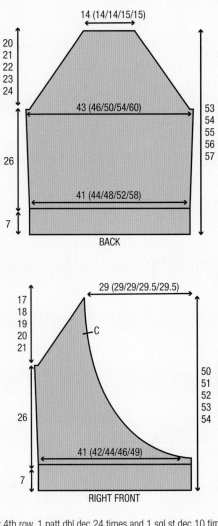

BACK

14 (14/14/15/15)

20
21
22
23
24

43 (46/50/54/60)

53
54
55
56
57

26

41 (44/48/52/58)

7

RIGHT FRONT

29 (29/29/29.5/29.5)

17
18
19
20
21

C

50
51
52
53
54

26

41 (42/44/46/49)

7

50-52: every 4th row, 1 patt dbl dec 24 times and 1 sgl st dec 10 times
When work measures 26cm from end of ribbing, shape raglan by casting off 2 sts at LH edge, then dec at 4th st from LH edge as follows
34-36: every 4th row, *1 patt dbl dec 3 times, 1 sgl st dec once*, rep from * to * 3 times in tot and foll 4th row, 1 patt dbl dec once
38-40: every 4th row, 1 patt dbl dec 14 times
42-44: every 4th row, 1 patt dbl dec 15 times
46-48: every 4th row, 1 patt dbl dec 9 times, foll alt row 1 patt dbl dec once, and every 4th row, 1 patt dbl dec 6 times
50-52: *every 4th row, 1 patt dbl dec 3 times, foll alt row 1 patt dbl dec once * rep from * to * 4 times in tot and finish with 1 patt dbl dec every 4th row, 3 times)
When work measures **43 (44, 45, 46, 47)** cm from end of ribbing, cast off rem 2 sts.
Make left front as for right, reversing all shaping.

Sleeveless wrap around top cont'd

RIGHT CAP SLEEVE

With 3.5mm needles, cast on **65 (72, 79, 86, 100)** sts and work in patt, starting and ending with 1 edge st.

When work measures 1cm, shape raglan by casting off 2 (2, 1, 1, 2) sts at each edge and then cast off at beg of each row as follows:

34-36: *1 st 10 times, work 2 rows straight then 1 st twice*, rep from * to * 4 times **(13 sts)**

38-40: *1 st 10 times, work 2 rows straight then 1 st twice*, rep from * to * 4 times in tot and then 1 st 6 times **(14 sts)**

42-44: 1 st 64 times **(13 sts)**

46-48: 1 st 70 times **(14 sts)**

50-52: *1 st 26 times then 2 sts twice*, rep from * to * twice and then 1 st 16 times **(20 sts)**

When work measures **18 (19, 20, 21, 22)** cm, cast off on both edges at same time as follows:

34-36: RH edge every alt row: 2 sts twice, 1 st 4 times and 2 sts once; LH edge 1 st on first row then 1 st every 4th row, twice

38-40: RH edge every alt row 3 sts once, 2 sts once, 1 st 3 times and 2 sts once; LH edge 1 st on first row then 1 st foll alt row, once, 1 st foll 4th row, once and 1 st foll alt row, once

42-44: RH edge every alt row 3 sts once, 2 sts once, 1 st 3 times and 2 sts once; LH edge 1 st on first row then 1 st every 4th row, twice

46-48: RH edge every alt row 2 sts twice, 1 st 3 times and 2 sts once; LH edge 1 st on first row then 1 st foll alt row, once, then every 4th row, 1 st once and 2 sts once

50-52: RH edge every alt row 3 sts twice, 2 sts once, 1 st 3 times and 2 sts once; LH edge 1 st on first row then 1 st every alt row, 4 times and 2 sts once.

Make left cap sleeve, reversing all shaping.

COLLAR

With 3mm needles, cast on **99 (99, 99, 103, 103)** sts and work 14cm in K1, P1 rib then work a K row on RS and a few rows of st st in another shade. Press these rows, they will be unpicked when sewing on the collar.

TIES

With 3mm needles, cast on 11 sts and work 40cm in K1, P1 rib, starting and ending first row and every odd row (RS) with K2 then cast off loosely. Knit an identical second tie.

RIGHT CAP SLEEVE

TO MAKE UP AND FINISH

Match cap sleeve raglan edges to body with shorter side at front. Join side and sleeve seams. Sew collar around neckline, st by st, using back stitch on RS of work and positioning ends at point marked C on patt. Sew end of one tie level with first dec row on right front edge. Sew end of second tie at side seam on left front.

6 Jacket

SIZES
34-36 (38-40, 42-44, 46-48, 50-52) (see Sizing Charts)

MATERIALS
Double knitting such as Zéphir from Phildar (36% wool, 36% acrylic and 28% polyamide): **10 (11, 12, 13, 14)** balls of main colour (M), shown here in Vison shade • Chunky weight yarn such as Neige from Phildar (100% polyamide): **1 (1, 1, 1, 1)** ball of contrast colour (A) shown in Chamois shade • Pair of 4mm, 5mm and 6mm needles • 4 press studs, 18mm in diameter • 2 cable needles

STITCHES USED
Garter stitch
Stocking stitch
Cable pattern stitch: see chart and legends
Right pleat: done over 21 sts:
Slip first 7 sts onto CN (CN1) and leave at back of work and slip next 7 sts onto another CN (CN2), also left at back of work but in front of CN1 (with RS of CN1 st st against RS of CN2 st st). Insert RHN into next st on LHN, then into a st on CN2 and first st on CN1, knit these 3 sts tog.
Do the same with the next 6 sts on each needle.
Left pleat: done over 21 sts:
Slip first 7 sts onto CN (CN1) and leave in front of work and slip next 7 sts onto another CN (CN2), also left in front of work but behind CN1 (with WS of CN1 st st against WS of CN2 st st). Insert RHN into first st on CN1, then into first st on CN2 and next st on LHN and knit these 3 sts tog. Do the same with the next 6 sts on each needle.

TENSION
It is essential to check your tension before starting your garment to ensure you get the right measurements.
On 4mm needles, 44 sts and 55 rows to 20cm in st st using double knitting yarn such as Zéphyr.
On 4mm needles, 32 sts and 28 rows to 10cm in patt using double knitting yarn such as Zéphyr.
On 6mm needles, 23 sts and 35 rows to 20cm in st st using Chunky yarn such as Neige.

INSTRUCTIONS
BACK
With 4mm needles, cast on **173 (178, 186, 196, 210)** sts using M (double knitting yarn) and work 2 rows of garter st (i.e. 1 ridge) then cont in st st. When work measures 11cm, form 4 pleats as follows:
knit **15 (16, 17, 20, 23)** sts, make one right pleat (see Stitches Used) with foll 21 sts, knit **16 (17, 19, 21, 24)** sts, make one right pleat (see Stitches Used) with foll 21 sts, knit **27 (28, 30, 30, 32)** sts, make one left pleat (see Stitches Used) with foll 21 sts, knit **16 (17, 19, 21, 24)** sts, make one left pleat (see Stitches Used) with foll 21 sts, knit **15 (16, 17, 20, 23)** sts.
117 (122, 130, 140, 154) sts remain.
Work 1 row purl.
Cont in patt and inc **31 (36, 45, 46, 50)** sts evenly on first row, setting patt as follows: P **4 (5, 5, 6, 6)**, *work 12 sts of panel patt (see chart) and P **4 (5, 5, 6, 6)***, rep from * to * **9 (9, 10, 10, 11)** times in tot.
148 (158, 175, 186, 204) sts.
Dec 1 st at each end of row as follows:
34-36, 38-40: every 16th row, 3 times and foll 14th row, once
42-44, 46-48: every 12th row, 3 times and every 10th row, 3 times
50-52: every 14th row, twice and every 12th row, 3 times). **140 (150, 163, 174, 194)** sts remain.
When work measures 27cm from pleats, shape armholes by casting off at beg of each row as follows:
34-36: 4 sts twice, 3 sts 4 times, 2 sts 4 times and 1 st twice
38-40: 4 sts twice, 3 sts 4 times, 2 sts 4 times and 1 st 6 times
42-44: 5 sts twice, 4 sts twice, 3 sts 4 times, 2 sts 4 times and 1 st 4 times
46-48: 5 sts twice, 4 sts 4 times, 3 sts 6 times, 2 sts 4 times and 1 st 6 times
50-52: 6 sts twice, 5 sts twice, 4 sts 4 times, 3 sts 6 times, 2 sts 4 times and 1 st 8 times. **110 (116, 121, 116, 122)** sts remain, with 1P (1P, 1P and 6 patt, 1 st and 6P, 1P) sts each side.
When work measures **46 (47, 48, 49, 50)** cm from pleats, shape shoulders by casting off at beg of every alt row at outside edge as follows: 6 sts twice and 7 sts twice (7 sts 3 times and 8 sts once, 8 sts 4 times, 7 sts 4 times, 7 sts once and 8 sts 3 times).
At the same time, shape neck by casting off the centre **20 (20, 19, 22, 22)** sts. Then cont, working one side at a time, casting off at neck edge every alt row: 10 sts once and 9 sts once.
Finish other side of neck, reversing shapings.

Jacket cont'd

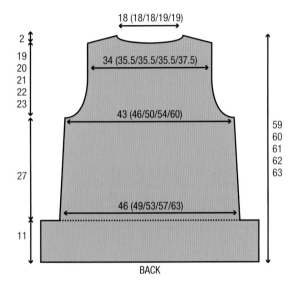

18 (18/18/19/19)

2
19
20
21
22
23

34 (35.5/35.5/35.5/37.5)

43 (46/50/54/60)

59
60
61
62
63

27

46 (49/53/57/63)

11

BACK

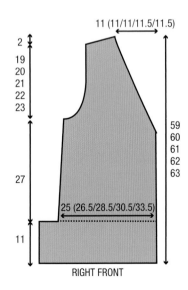

11 (11/11/11.5/11.5)

2
19
20
21
22
23

59
60
61
62
63

27

25 (26.5/28.5/30.5/33.5)

11

RIGHT FRONT

RIGHT FRONT

With 4mm needles, cast on **92 (95, 99, 104, 111)** sts using M and work 2 rows of garter st (i.e. 1 ridge) then cont in st st.

When work measures 11cm, form 2 pleats as follows:

knit **19 (20, 21, 21, 22)** sts, make one left pleat (see Stitches Used) with foll 21 sts, knit **16 (17, 19, 21, 24)** sts, make one left pleat (see Stitches Used) with foll 21 sts, knit **15 (16, 17, 20, 23)** sts.

64 (67, 71, 76, 83) sts remain.

Work 1 row purl.

Cont in patt and inc **18 (20, 19, 19, 27)** sts evenly on first row, setting patt as follows: P**2 (2, 5, 5, 2)**, *work 12 sts of panel patt (see chart) and P**4 (5, 5, 6, 6)***, rep from * to * **5 (5, 5, 5, 6)** times in tot. **82 (87, 90, 95, 110)** sts.

Cast off 1 st at LH edge as follows:

34-36, 38-40: every 16th row, 3 times and foll 14th row, once

42-44, 46-48: every 12th row, 3 times and every 10th row, 3 times

50-52: every 14th row, twice and every 12th row, 3 times

Meanwhile, when work measures **23 (24, 25, 26, 27)** cm from pleats, shape neck. Cast off at RH edge as follows:

34-36, 38-40: 2 sts once then on every alt row 2 sts once and 1 st 33 times

42-44: 1st once then on every alt row 1st 28 times and every 4th row, 1st 5 times

46-48: 1st once then on every alt row 1st 16 times and every 4th row 1st 11 times

50-52: 2 sts once then on every alt row 2 sts twice and 1st 32 times.

When work measures 27cm from pleats, shape armhole by casting off at LH edge on every alt row as follows:

34-36: 4 sts once, 3 sts twice, 2 sts twice and 1st once

38-40: 4 sts once, 3 sts twice, 2 sts twice and 1st 3 times

42-44: 5 sts once, 4 sts once, 3 sts twice, 2 sts twice and 1st twice

46-48: 5 sts once, 4 sts twice, 3 sts 3 times, 2 sts twice and 1st 3 times

50-52: 6 sts once, 5 sts once, 4 sts twice, 3 sts 3 times, 2 sts twice and 1st 4 times.

When work measures **46 (47, 48, 49, 50)** cm from pleats, shape shoulder by casting off at armhole edge every alt row as follows:

6 sts twice and 7 sts twice (7 sts 3 times and 8 sts once, 8 sts 4 times, 7 sts 4 times, 7 sts once and 8 sts 3 times).

Make left front, reversing shaping.

TO MAKE UP AND FINISH

Join shoulder, side and sleeve seams. Sew sleeves into armholes. With 5mm needles and A (Chunky yarn such as Neige from Phildar), pick up **95 (95, 95, 99, 99)** sts around neckline starting at first neck dec row on front pieces. Change to 6mm needles and work in rev st st, working short rows as follows: leave 2 sts unworked at each end of row and then leave another 2 sts unworked each end every alt row **17 (17, 17, 18, 18)** times. Work one row across all sts and cast off loosely. Sew press studs along front edges, the first at bottom of collar and the others evenly spaced.

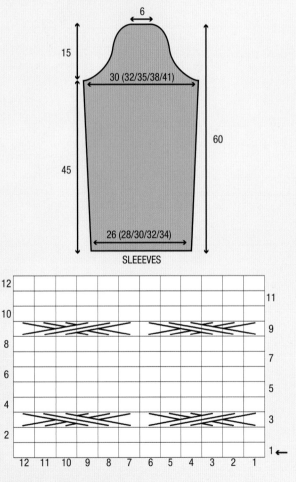

SLEEEVES

12 11

10

8 9

6 7

4 5

2 3

1 ←

12 11 10 9 8 7 6 5 4 3 2 1

SLEEVES

With 4mm needles, cast on **84 (90, 98, 104, 110)** sts using M and work in patt as follows:

34-36: P4, *work 12 sts of panel patt, P4*, rep from * to * 5 times in tot

38-40: P5, *work 12 sts of panel patt, P5*, rep from * to * 5 times in tot

42-44: K4, P5, *work 12 sts of panel patt, P5*, rep from * to * 5 times in tot and then K4,

46-48: K4, P6, *work 12 sts of panel patt, P6*, rep from * to * 5 times in tot and then K4

50-52: K7, P6, *work 12 sts of panel patt, P6*, rep from * to * 5 times in tot and then K7).

Inc 1 st each end, incorporating sts into patt: every 16th row 7 times (every 16th row 7 times; every 14th row 8 times; every 12th row 8 times and every 10th row twice; every 10th row 11 times and foll 8th row once).

98 (104, 114, 124, 134) sts.

When work measures 45cm, shape by casting off at beg of each row as follows:

34-36: 3 sts twice, 2 sts 14 times, 1 st 12 times, 2 sts 12 times and 3 sts twice

38-40: 3 sts 4 times, 2 sts 12 times, 1 st 10 times, 2 sts 12 times and 3 sts 4 times

42-44: 3 sts 6 times, 2 sts 14 times, 1 st 4 times, 2 sts 12 times and 3 sts 6 times

46-48: 3 sts 10 times, 2 sts 10 times, 1 st twice, 2 sts 10 times, 3 sts 10 times

50-52: 3 sts 14 times, 2 sts 14 times and 3 sts 14 times

Cont until work measures 60cm then cast off rem 22 sts.

Knit second sleeve to match.

☐ K on RS; P on WS

⟩⟩≫≪⟨⟨ C6F: slip next 3 sts onto cable needle and leave at front of work, K3 from left hand needle then K3 from cable needle

⟩⟩≫≪⟨⟨ C6B: slip next 3 sts onto cable needle and leave at back of work, K3 from left hand needle then K3 from cable needle

7
Belted top

Fair Isle and rib.
Sport weight such as
Partner 3.5.

7 *Belted top*

SIZES

34-36 (38-40, 42-44, 46-48, 50-52) (see Sizing Charts)

MATERIALS

5-ply or Sport weight yarn such as Partner 3.5 from Phildar (50% polyamide, 25% worsted wool and 25% acrylic): **7 (8, 8, 9, 10)** balls of main colour (M), shown here in Châtaigne; **1 (1, 1, 2, 2)** balls of contrast colour (A), shown here in Poudre • Pair each 3mm and 3.5mm needles • 1 belt buckle

STITCHES USED

K1, P1 rib
Stocking stitch
Fair Isle patt worked in st st: see chart and legends

TENSION

It is essential to check your tension before starting your garment to ensure you get the right measurements.
On 3.5mm needles, 24 sts and 30 rows to 10cm in st st and Fair Isle.

INSTRUCTIONS

BACK

With 3mm needles, cast on **106 (112, 122, 132, 146)** sts using M and work 5cm in K1, P1 rib.

Change to 3.5mm needles and cont in st st, using M. Dec 1 in the 3rd st from each end of row, as follows: every 8th row twice and every 6th row 4 times (every 8th row 5 times; every 8th row 5 times; every 10th row 3 times and foll 8th row once; every 8th row, 5 times).

94 (102, 112, 124, 136) sts remain.

Cont until work measures 15cm from end of ribbing then inc 1 in 3rd st from each end of foll row and then rep as follows:

34-36: every 10th row 3 times and every 8th row twice

38-40, 42-44, 50-52: every 12th row twice and every 10th row twice

46-48: every 14th row 3 times. **106 (112, 122, 132, 146)** sts.

When work measures 33cm from end of ribbing, shape armholes by inc 1 st each end of foll row and rep as follows:

34-36: every 4th row 7 times and every 6th row 4 times **(130 sts)**

38-40: every 4th row 6 times and every 6th row 5 times **(136 sts)**

42-44: every 4th row 4 times and every 6th row 7 times **(146 sts)**

46-48: every 4th row 3 times and every 6th row 8 times **(156 sts)**

50-52: foll 4th row once and every 6th row 10 times **(170 sts)**

When work measures **52 (53, 54, 55, 56)** cm from end of ribbing, shape shoulders by casting off at beg of every alt row at outside edge as follows: 10 sts 3 times and 11 sts once (11 sts 4 times; 12 sts 3 times and 13 sts once; 13 sts 3 times and 14 sts once; 15 sts 4 times).

At the same time, shape neck by casting off the centre **16 (16, 16, 18, 18)** sts then cont, working one side at a time and cast off 8 sts at neck edge every alt row, twice. Finish other side of neck, matching all shaping.

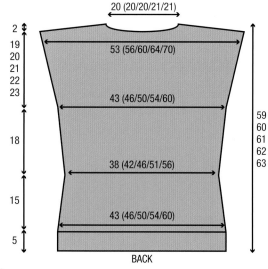

BACK

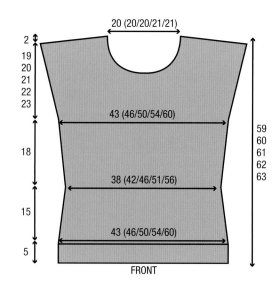

FRONT

FRONT

With 3mm needles, cast on **106 (112, 122, 132, 146)** sts using M and work 5cm in K1, P1 rib.

Change to 3.5mm needles and cont in st st following Fair Isle spotted patt on chart. Dec 1 in the 3rd st from each end of row, as follows:

34-36: every 8th row twice and every 6th row 4 times

38-40, 42-44, 50-52: every 8th row, 5 times

46-48: every 10th row 3 times and foll 8th row once. **94 (102, 112, 124, 136)** sts remain.

When work measures 15cm from end of ribbing, inc 1 in 3rd st from each end of foll row and then repeat as follows:

34-36: every 10th row 3 times and every 8th row twice

38-40, 42-44, 50-52: every 12th row twice and every 10th row twice

46-48: every 14th row 3 times. **106 (112, 122, 132, 146)** sts.

When work measures 33cm from end of ribbing, shape armholes by inc 1 st each end of foll row and rep as follows:

34-36: every 4th row 7 times and every 6th row 4 times **(130 sts)**

38-40: every 4th row 6 times and every 6th row 5 times **(136 sts)**

42-44: every 4th row 4 times and every 6th row 7 times **(146 sts)**

46-48: every 4th row 3 times and every 6th row 8 times **(156 sts)**

50-52: foll 4th row once and every 6th row 10 times **(170 sts)**

When work measures **44 (45, 46, 47, 48)** cm from end of ribbing, shape neck by casting off the centre **14 (14, 14, 16, 16)** sts then cont, working one side at a time and cast off at neck edge every alt row as follows on all sizes: 4 sts once, 3 sts once, 2 sts twice, 1 st 3 times and then 1 st every 4th row, 3 times (17 sts in total).

When work measures **52 (53, 54, 55, 56)** cm from end of ribbing, shape shoulder by casting off at armhole edge every alt row as follows: 10 sts 3 times and 11 sts once (11 sts 4 times; 12 sts 3 times and 13 sts once; 13 sts 3 times and 14 sts once; 15 sts 4 times).

Finish other side of neck.

Belted top cont'd

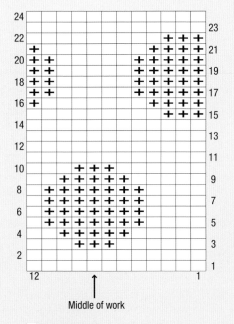

Middle of work

☐ Main colour (M)
+ Contrast colour (A)

COLLAR

With 3mm needles cast on **142 (142, 142, 146, 146)** sts using M and work 8cm in K1, P1 rib. Work short rows, putting 9 sts on holder at each end every alt row, 5 times, then work one row across all sts.

Work a few rows in st st in another shade. Press these rows, they will be unpicked when sewing on the collar.

BELT

With 3mm needles, cast on 13 sts using M and work **91 (95, 99, 104, 109)** cm in K1, P1 rib, starting and ending first row and every odd row (RS) with K2 then cast off loosely in rib.

TO MAKE UP AND FINISH

Join shoulder and side seams.

Sew collar around neckline, st by st, using back stitch on RS of work and positioning ends of collar in middle of front neckline.

Using M, cover belt buckle by wrapping yarn around it.

Fold 2cm of belt over buckle and attach with concealed stitching.

8
Sleeveless top

Stocking stitch and K1, P1 rib.
4-ply such as Pur Angora and Sunset.

9
Cardigan

Stocking stitch and K1, P1 rib.
4-ply such as Pur Angora
and Sunset.

8 Sleeveless top

SIZES
34-36 (38-40, 42-44, 46-48, 50-52) (see Sizing Charts)

MATERIALS
4-ply such as Pur Angora from Phildar (100% angora): **6 (6, 7, 7, 8)** balls of main colour (M), shown here in Biche • 4-ply such as Sunset from Phildar (65% viscose and 35% polyester): **1 (1, 1, 1, 2)** balls of contrast colour (A), shown here in Irisé • Pair of 3.5mm needles

STITCHES USED
K1, P1 rib
Stocking stitch

TENSION
It is essential to check your tension before starting your garment to ensure you get the right measurements.
On 3.5mm needles, 25 sts and 30 rows to 10cm in st st using 4-ply yarn such as Pur Angora.

INSTRUCTIONS
BACK
With 3.5mm needles, cast on **104 (112, 122, 132, 148)** sts using 1 strand of M and 1 strand of A knitted together. Work 5cm in K1, P1 rib, starting and ending first row and every odd row (RS) with K1.

Still using 3.5mm needles, cont in st st, using M only and dec 1 in 3rd st from each end of row as follows: every 12th row 3 times (every 16th row twice; every 16th row twice; foll 24th row once; every 12th row 3 times). **98 (108, 118, 130, 142)** sts remain.

When work measures 15cm from end of ribbing, inc 1 in 3rd st from each end of foll row, then repeat as follows:
34-36: every 8th row 5 times and every 6th row twice
38-40: foll 10th row once and every 8th row 5 times
42-44: foll 10th row once and every 8th row 5 times
46-48: every 10th row 5 times
50-52: every 8th row 5 times and every 6th row, twice. **114 (122, 132, 142, 158)** sts.

When work measures 34cm from end of ribbing, shape armholes by casting off at beg of each row as follows:
34-36: 4 sts twice, 3 sts 4 times, 2 sts 4 times and 1 st 4 times
38-40: 5 sts twice, 4 sts twice, 3 sts 4 times, 2 sts twice and 1 st 4 times
42-44: 5 sts twice, 4 sts twice, 3 sts 4 times, 2 sts 4 times and 1 st 6 times
46-48: 5 sts twice, 4 sts 4 times, 3 sts 4 times, 2 sts 4 times and 1 st 6 times
50-52: 5 sts 4 times, 4 sts 4 times, 3 sts 4 times, 2 sts 6 times and 1 st 6 times.
82 (84, 88, 90, 92) sts remain.

When work measures **52 (53, 54, 55, 56)** cm from end of ribbing, shape shoulders by casting off at beg of every alt row at outside edge as follows: 3 sts 3 times and 4 sts once (3 sts twice and 4 sts twice; 4 sts 4 times; 4 sts 4 times; 4 sts 3 times and 5 sts once).

At the same time, shape neck by casting off the centre **22 (22, 22, 24, 24)** sts and cont, working one side at a time, casting off at neck edge every alt row: 9 sts once and 8 sts once.
Finish other side of neck, matching shaping.

FRONT
With 3.5mm needles, cast on **104 (112, 122, 132, 148)** sts using 1 strand of M and 1 strand of A knitted together. Work 5cm in K1, P1 rib, starting and ending first row and every odd row (RS) with K1.

Still using 3.5mm needles, cont in st st, using M. Dec 1 in the 3rd st from each end of row, as follows: every 12th row, 3 times (every 16th row twice; every 16th row twice; foll 24th row once; every 12th row 3 times). **98 (108, 118, 130, 142)** sts remain.

When work measures 15cm from end of ribbing, inc 1 in 3rd st from each end of foll row, then repeat as follows:
34-36, 50-52: every 8th row 5 times and every 6th row twice
38-40, 42-44: foll 10th row once and every 8th row 5 times

46-48: every 10th row 5 times. **114 (122, 132, 142, 158)** sts.
When work measures 34cm from end of ribbing, shape armholes by casting off at beg of each row as follows:
34-36: 4 sts twice, 3 sts 4 times, 2 sts 4 times and 1 st 4 times
38-40: 5 sts twice, 4 sts twice, 3 sts 4 times, 2 sts twice and 1 st 4 times
42-44: 5 sts twice, 4 sts twice, 3 sts 4 times, 2 sts 4 times and 1 st 6 times
46-48: 5 sts twice, 4 sts 4 times, 3 sts 4 times, 2 sts 4 times and 1 st 6 times
50-52: 5 sts 4 times, 4 sts 4 times, 3 sts 4 times, 2 sts 6 times and 1 st
6 times
82 (84, 88, 90, 92) sts remain.
When work measures **41 (42, 43, 44, 45)** cm from end of ribbing, shape neck by casting off the centre **20 (20, 20, 22, 22)** sts then cont to work one side at a time and dec at neck edge on every alt row as follows for all sizes: 3 sts twice, 2 sts twice, 1 st twice then 1 st every 4th row, 6 times **(18 sts)**.
When work measures **52 (53, 54, 55, 56)** cm from end of ribbing, shape shoulder by casting off at armhole edge every alt row as follows: 3 sts 3 times and 4 sts once (3 sts twice and 4 sts twice; 4 sts 4 times; 4 sts 4 times; 4 sts 3 times and 5 sts once).
Finish other side of neck, matching shaping.

NECKBAND
With 3.5mm needles, cast on **170 (170, 170, 174, 174)** sts using 1 strand of M and 1 strand of A, knitted together and work 2cm in K1, P1 rib.
Do one K row on RS and a few rows of st st in another shade.
Press these rows, they will be unpicked when attaching the neckband.

ARMHOLE BANDS
With 3.5mm needles, cast on **86 (90, 94, 98, 102)** sts. using 1 strand of M and 1 strand of A, knitted together and work 2cm in K1, P1 rib.
Do one K row on RS and a few rows of st st in another shade.
Press these rows, they will be unpicked when attaching the armhole bands.
Knit second band to match.

TO MAKE UP AND FINISH
Join shoulder and side seams.
Sew on the neckband, st by st, using back st, on the RS of work.
Sew on the armhole bands, st by st, using back st, on the RS of work.

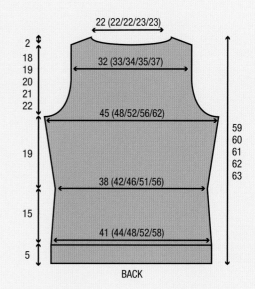

BACK

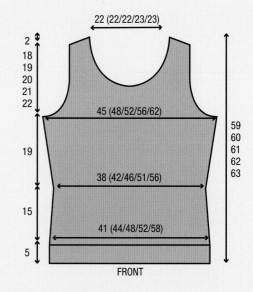

FRONT

37

9 Cardigan

SIZES
34-36 (38-40, 42-44, 46-48, 50-52) (see Sizing Charts)

MATERIALS
4-ply such as Pur Angora from Phildar (100% angora): **8 (9, 10, 11, 12)** balls of main colour (M) shown here in Biche • 4-ply such as Sunset from Phildar (65% viscose and 35% polyester): **1 (1, 1, 2, 2)** balls of contrast colour (A), shown here in Irisé • Pair of 3.5mm needles • 7 Buttons

STITCHES USED
K1, P1 rib
Stocking stitch

TENSION
It is essential to check your tension before starting your garment to ensure you get the right measurements.
On 3.5mm needles, 25 sts and 30 rows to 10cm in st st using 4-ply yarn such as Pur Angora.

INSTRUCTIONS
BACK
With 3.5mm needles, cast on **109 (117, 127, 137, 151)** sts using 1 strand of M and 1 strand of A knitted together. Work 5cm in K1, P1 rib, starting and ending first row and every odd row (RS) with K1.

Still using 3.5mm needles, cont in st st with M on its own. Dec 1 in the 3rd st from each end of row, as follows: every 8th row twice and every 6th row 4 times (every 8th row 5 times; every 8th row 5 times; every 10th row 3 times and foll 8th row once; every 8th row 5 times).

97 (107, 117, 129, 141) sts remain.

When work measures 15cm from end of ribbing, inc 1 in 3rd st from each end of next row and then rep as follows: every 14th row 3 times (every 18th row twice; every 18th row twice; foll 28th row once; every 18th row twice).

105 (113, 123, 133, 147) sts.

When work measures 33cm from end of ribbing, shape armholes by casting off at beg of each row as follows:

34-36: 3 sts twice, 2 sts 4 times and 1 st 6 times
38-40: 4 sts twice, 3 sts twice, 2 sts 4 times and 1 st 4 times
42-44: 4 sts twice, 3 sts 4 times, 2 sts 4 times and 1 st 6 times
46-48: 5 sts twice, 4 sts twice, 3 sts 4 times, 2 sts 4 times and 1 st 4 times
50-52: 5 sts twice, 4 sts 4 times, 3 sts 4 times, 2 sts 4 times and 1 st 6 times

85 (87, 89, 91, 95) sts remain.

When work measures **52 (53, 54, 55, 56)** cm from end of ribbing, shape shoulders by casting off at beg of every alt row at outside edge as follows: 3 sts once and 4 sts 3 times (4 sts 4 times; 4 sts 3 times and 5 sts once; 4 sts 3 times and 5 sts once; 4 sts once and 5 sts 3 times).

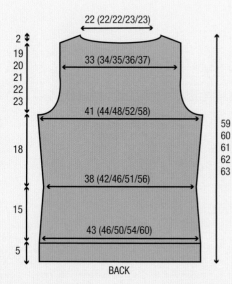

BACK

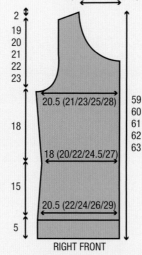

RIGHT FRONT

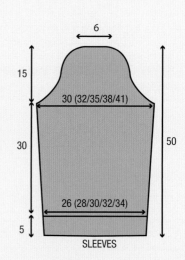

SLEEVES

At the same time, shape neck by casting off the centre **21 (21, 21, 23, 23)** sts and cont, working one side at a time, casting off at neck edge every alt row: 9 sts once and 8 sts once.
Finish other side of neck matching shapings.

RIGHT FRONT

With 3.5mm needles, cast on **53 (57, 63, 67, 75)** sts, using 1 strand of M and 1 strand of A knitted together. Work 5cm in K1, P1 rib, starting first row and every odd row (RS) with K2 and ending with P1.
Still using 3.5mm needles, cont in st st, and use M on its own. Dec 1 in the 3rd st from LH edge as follows: every 8th row twice and every 6th row 4 times (every 8th row 5 times; every 8th row 5 times; every 10th row 3 times and foll 8th row once; every 8th row 5 times). **47 (52, 58, 63, 70)** sts remain.
When work measures 15cm from end of ribbing, inc 1 in 3rd st from LH edge in foll row then repeat as follows: every 14th row 3 times (every 18th row twice; every 18th row twice; foll 28th row once; every 18th row twice).
51 (55, 61, 65, 73) sts.
When work measures 33cm from end of ribbing, shape armhole by casting off at LH edge every alt row as follows:
34-36: 3 sts once, 2 sts twice and 1 st 3 times
38-40: 4 sts once, 3 sts once, 2 sts twice and 1 st twice
42-44: 4 sts once, 3 sts twice, 2 sts twice and 1 st 3 times
46-48: 5 sts once, 4 sts once, 3 sts twice, 2 sts twice and 1 st twice
50-52: 5 sts once, 4 sts twice, 3 sts twice, 2 sts twice and 1 st 3 times
41 (42, 44, 44, 47) sts remain.
When work measures **43 (44, 45, 46, 47)** cm from end of ribbing, shape neck by casting off at RH edge every alt row as follows:
34-36, 38-40: 5 sts once, 4 sts once, 3 sts twice, 2 sts twice, 1 st 4 times, then every 4th row, 1st 3 times
42-44, 46-48: 5 sts once, 4 sts once, 3 sts twice, 2 sts twice, 1 st 6 times, then every 4th row, 1 st twice

50-52: 5 sts once, 4 sts once, 3 sts twice, 2 sts twice, 1 st 8 times, then 1st on foll 4th row once
When work measures **52 (53, 54, 55, 56)** cm from end of ribbing, shape shoulder by casting off at armhole edge every alt row as follows: 3 sts once and 4 sts 3 times (4 sts 4 times; 4 sts 3 times and 5 sts once; 4 sts 3 times and 5 sts once; 4 sts once and 5 sts 3 times).
Make left front, reversing shaping.

SLEEVES

With 3.5mm needles, cast on **68 (72, 78, 82, 88)** sts using 1 strand of M and 1 strand of A, knitted together and work 5cm in K1, P1 rib.
Still using 3.5mm needles, cont in st st and use M only. Inc 1 in the 3rd st from each end of row, as follows: every 16th row 3 times and every 14th row twice (every 16th row 3 times and every 14th row twice; every 14th row 3 times and every 12th row 3 times; every 10th row 8 times; every 10th row 8 times).
78 (82, 90, 98, 104) sts.
When work measures 30cm from end of ribbing, shape by casting off at beg of each row as follows:
34-36: 2 sts 8 times, 1 st 14 times, work 2 rows straight then 1 st 14 times and 2 sts 8 times
38-40: 2 sts 10 times, 1 st 12 times, work 2 rows straight then 1 st 12 times and 2 sts 10 times
42-44: 3 sts twice, 2 sts 10 times, 1 st 10 times, work 2 rows straight then 1 st 10 times. 2 sts 10 times and 3 sts twice
46-48: 3 sts 4 times, 2 sts 10 times, 1 st 8 times, work 2 rows straight and then 1 st 8 times, 2 sts 10 times and 3 sts 4 times
50-52: 3 sts 6 times, 2 sts 8 times, 1 st 18 times, 2 sts 8 times and 3 sts 6 times.
When work measures 45cm from end of ribbing, loosely cast off rem 18 sts.
Knit second sleeve to match.

NECKBAND

With 3.5mm needles cast on **159 (159, 159, 163, 163)** sts using 1 strand of M and 1 strand of A knitted together. Work 2cm in K1, P1 rib, starting and ending first row and every odd row (RS) with K2. Do one K row on RS and a few rows of st st in another shade. Press these rows, they will be unpicked when attaching neckband.

BUTTONBAND

With 3.5mm needles, cast on **125 (127, 129, 133, 135)** sts using 1 strand of M and 1 strand of A knitted together. Work 2cm in K1, P1 rib, starting and ending first row and every odd row (RS) with K2. Do one K row on RS and a few rows of st st in another shade.
Press these rows, they will be unpicked when attaching band.
Make buttonhole band in same way but make 7 buttonholes over 2 sts on 4th row, positioning first buttonhole **4 (3, 3, 3, 3)** sts from edge and the rest spaced **17 (18, 18, 19, 19)** sts apart.

TO MAKE UP AND FINISH

Join shoulder, side and sleeve seams. Sew sleeves into armholes. Sew on the neckband, st by st, using back st, on RS of work.
Sew buttonband and buttonhole band to front edges and neckband. Sew on buttons.

The '60s

Miniskirts and geometric designs, inspired by Courrèges and Cardin or maybe "The Avengers"

10 Zip-up cardigan

Stocking stitch and K1, P1 rib.
Aran weight yarn such as Phil Harmony.

11 Sweater

Stocking stitch and K1, P1 rib.
Aran weight yarn such as Iliade.

12 Skirt

Intarsia colourwork with ribbed edging.
Aran weight yarn such as Iliade.

10 Zip-up cardigan

SIZES
S (15-17yrs), M (42-44), L (46-48), XL (50-52), XXL (54-56) (see Sizing Charts)

MATERIALS
Aran weight yarn such as Phil Harmony from Phildar (51% wool and 49% acrylic): **11 (12, 14, 15, 16)** balls of main colour (M) shown here in Noir; **1 (1, 2, 2, 2)** balls of contrast colour (A), shown in Myrtille • 1 x **60 (65, 65, 65, 65)** cm zip • 7cm of petersham to match M • 1 button, 18mm in diameter • Pair each 5mm and 5.5mm needles

STITCHES USED
K1, P1 rib
Stocking stitch

TENSION
It is essential to check your tension before starting your garment to ensure you get the right measurements.
On 5.5mm needles, 15 sts and 23 rows to 10cm in st st.

INSTRUCTIONS
BACK
With 5mm needles, cast on **71 (75, 81, 87, 93)** sts using A and work 3cm in K1, P1 rib then do 1 P row on WS.
Change to 5.5mm needles and cont in st st, using M.
When work measures 41cm from end of ribbing, shape armholes by casting off at beg of each row as follows: 3 sts twice, 2 sts twice and 1 st 6 times (3 sts twice, 2 sts twice and 1 st 6 times ;3 sts 4 times, 2 sts twice and 1 st 4 times; 3 sts 4 times, 2 sts twice and 1 st 4 times; 3 sts 4 times, 2 sts 4 times and 1 st twice). **55 (59, 61, 67, 71)** sts remain.
When work measures **61 (62, 63, 64, 65)** cm from end of ribbing, shape shoulders by casting off at beg of every alt row at outside edge as follows: 5 sts 3 times (5 sts twice and 6 sts once; 5 sts once and 6 sts twice; 6 sts twice and 7 sts once; 7 sts 3 times).
At the same time, shape neck by casting off the centre **9 (11, 11, 13, 13)** sts then cont, working one side at a time, casting off 8 sts at neck edge on foll alt row.
Finish other side of neck, matching shaping.

RIGHT FRONT
With 5mm needles, cast on **37 (39, 41, 44, 47)** sts using A and work 3cm in K1, P1 rib, starting first row with K2. Do 1 P row on WS.
Change to 5.5mm needles, cont in st st using M and dec **1 (1, 0, 0, 0)** st.
36 (38, 41, 44, 47) sts remain.
When work measures 41cm from end of ribbing, shape armhole by casting off at LH edge every alt row as follows: 3 sts once, 2 sts once and 1 st 3 times (3 sts once, 2 sts once and 1 st 3 times; 3 sts twice, 2 sts once and 1 st twice; 3 sts twice, 2 sts once and 1 st twice; 3 sts twice, 2 sts twice and 1 st once).
28 (30, 31, 34, 36) sts remain.
When work measures **55 (56, 57, 58, 58)** cm from end of ribbing, shape neck by casting off at RH edge every alt row: 4 sts once, 3 sts once, 2 sts once and 1st 4 times (4 sts once, 3 sts once, 2 sts twice, 1st twice and 1st on foll 4th row; 4 sts once, 3 sts once, 2 sts twice, 1st twice and 1st on foll 4th row; 4 sts once, 3 sts once, 2 sts twice and 1st 4 times; 4 sts once, 3 sts once, 2 sts twice, 1st 3 times and 1st on foll 4th row once).
When work measures **61 (62, 63, 64, 65)** cm from end of ribbing, shape shoulder by casting off at armhole edge every alt row as follows: 5 sts 3 times (5 sts twice and 6 sts once; 5 sts once and 6 sts twice; 6 sts twice and 7 sts once; 7 sts 3 times).

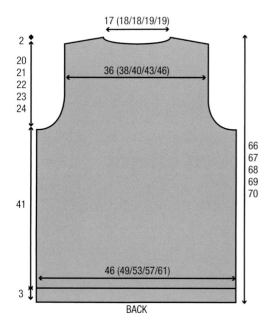

17 (18/18/19/19)

2

20
21
22
23
24

36 (38/40/43/46)

66
67
68
69
70

41

46 (49/53/57/61)

3

BACK

LEFT FRONT

With 5mm needles, cast on **37 (39, 41, 44, 47)** sts using A and work 3cm in
K1, P1 rib, starting first row with K2. Do 1 P row on WS.
Change to 5.5mm needles, cont in st st using M and dec **1 (1, 0, 0, 0)** st.
36 (38, 41, 44, 47) sts remain.
When work measures 41cm from end of ribbing, shape armhole by casting off
at RH edge every alt row: 3 sts once, 2 sts once and 1st 3 times (3 sts once, 2
sts once and 1st 3 times; 3 sts twice, 2 sts once and 1 st twice; 3 sts twice, 2
sts once and 1 st twice; 3 sts twice, 2 sts twice and 1 st once).
28 (30, 31, 34, 36) sts remain.
When work measures **44 (45, 46, 47, 48)** cm from end of ribbing, cont in st st,
using Fair Isle or intarsia stranded colourwork technique as follows: **3 (5, 6, 9,
11)** sts in M, 15 sts in A, 10 sts in M.
When work measures **45 (46, 47, 48, 49)** cm from end of ribbing, work **3 (5, 6,
9, 11)** sts, cast off foll 15 sts and work last 10 sts.
On next row, work 10 sts in M, pick up 15 sts in A and work **3 (5, 6, 9, 11)** sts
in M.
Work 4 rows then cont in st st, using M on all sts.
When work measures **55 (56, 57, 58, 58)** cm from end of ribbing, shape neck
by casting off at LH edge every alt row as follows:
S: 4 sts once, 3 sts once, 2 sts once and 1 st 4 times
M: 4 sts once, 3 sts once, 2 sts
twice, 1 st twice and 1 st on foll
4th row
L: 4 sts once, 3 sts once, 2 sts
twice, 1 st twice and 1 st on foll
4th row
XL: 4 sts once, 3 sts once, 2 sts
twice and 1 st 4 times
XXL: 4 sts once, 3 sts once, 2
sts twice, 1 st 3 times and 1 st
on foll 4th row once.
When work measures **61 (62,
63, 64, 65)** cm from end of ribbing, shape shoulder by casting
off at armhole edge every alt
row as follows: 5 sts 3 times
(5 sts twice and 6 sts once; 5
sts once and 6 sts twice; 6 sts
twice and 7 sts once; 7 sts 3
times).

8.5 (9/9/9.5/9.5)

2

20
21
22
23
24

18 (19/20/21.5/23)

66
67
68
69
70

41

24 (24.5/26.5/28.5/30.5)

3

RIGHT FRONT

The '60s

Zip-up cardigan cont'd

SLEEVES

With 5mm needles, cast on **36 (38, 42, 44, 48)** sts using A and work 3cm in K1, P1 rib, then do 1 P row on WS.

Change to 5.5mm needles and cont in st st using M. Inc 1 in the 3rd st from each end of row, as follows: every 12th row 4 times and every 10th row 5 times (every 10th row 10 times; every 12th row 4 times and every 10th row 5 times; every 10th row 10 times; every 12th row 4 times and every 10th row 5 times). **54 (58, 60, 64, 66)** sts.

When work measures 47cm from end of ribbing, shape by casting off at beg of each row as follows:

S: 2 sts 4 times, 1 st 10 times, work 2 rows straight then 1 st twice, work 2 rows st then 1 st 12 times and 2 sts 4 times

M: 2 sts 6 times, 1 st 10 times, work 2 rows straight then 1 st 14 times and 2 sts 4 times

L: 2 sts 6 times, 1 st 10 times, work 2 rows straight then 1 st 12 times and 2 sts 6 times

XL: 2 sts 8 times, 1 st 8 times, work 2 rows straight then 1 st 10 times and 2 sts 8 times

XXL: 3 sts twice, 2 sts 6 times, 1 st 8 times, work 2 rows straight then 1 st 10 times and 2 sts 8 times

When work measures 63cm from end of ribbing, loosely cast off rem 14 sts. Knit second sleeve to match.

COLLAR

With 5mm needles, cast on **79 (83, 83, 87, 87)** sts using A and work in K1, P1 rib, starting first row and every odd row (RS) with K2.

When work measures 3cm in tot, switch to M and cont in K1, P1 rib until work measures **10 (12, 10, 10, 10)** cm. Do a K row on RS and a few rows of st st in another shade.

Press these rows, they will be unpicked when attaching collar.

POCKET LINING

With 5.5mm needles, cast on 17 sts using M. Work 10cm in st st then cast off loosely.

TO MAKE UP AND FINISH

Join shoulder, side and sleeve seams. Sew sleeves into armholes. Sew on the collar, st by st, using back st, on RS of work. Fold collar in half, towards the inside of the cardigan and sew in place with concealed stitching. Sew pocket lining to WS of work using concealed stitching. Sew zip to front edges and collar edges, leaving top **2 (0, 0, 1, 1)** cm of collar free. Stitch petersham in middle of breast pocket and stitch button to petersham to close (see photo).

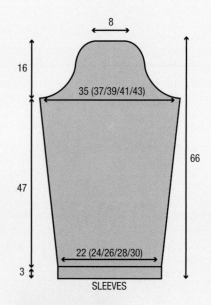

8

16

35 (37/39/41/43)

66

47

22 (24/26/28/30)

3

SLEEVES

11 Sweater

SIZES
34-36 (38-40, 42-44, 46-48, 50-52) (see Sizing Charts)

MATERIALS
Aran weight yarn such as lliade from Phildar (70% acrylic and 30% wool):
4 (4, 5, 5, 6) balls of main colour (M) shown here in Noir; **2 (3, 3, 3, 3)** balls
of contrast colour (A), shown in Blanc • Pair each 4mm and 4.5mm needles

STITCHES USED
K1, P1 rib
Stocking stitch

TENSION
It is essential to check your tension before starting your garment to ensure you
get the right measurements.
On 4.5mm needles, 19 sts and 27 rows to 10cm in st st.

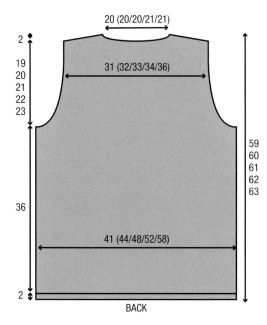

BACK

INSTRUCTIONS
BACK
With 4mm needles, cast on **80 (86, 94, 100, 112)** sts using M and work 2cm
in K1, P1 rib.

Change to 4.5mm needles and cont in st st still using M.

When work measures 34cm from end of ribbing, change to A and cont in st
st until work measures 36cm from end of ribbing. Shape armholes by casting
off at beg of each row as follows: 4 sts twice, 3 sts twice, 2 sts twice and 1 st
twice (4 sts twice, 3 sts twice, 2 sts twice and 1 st 6 times, 4 sts twice, 3 sts
4 times, 2 sts 4 times and 1 st twice, 4 sts twice, 3 sts 4 times, 2 sts 4 times
and 1 st 6 times, 5 sts twice, 4 sts twice, 3 sts 4 times, 2 sts 4 times and 1 st
4 times). **60 (62, 64, 66, 70)** sts remain.

When work measures **55 (56, 57, 58, 59)** cm from end of ribbing, shape
shoulders by casting off at beg of every alt row at outside edge as follows:
2 sts once and 3 sts 3 times (3 sts 4 times; 3 sts 3 times and 4 sts once; 3 sts
3 times and 4 sts once; 3 sts once and 4 sts 3 times).

At the same time, shape neck by casting off the centre **14 (14, 14, 16, 16)**
sts and cont, working one side at a time, casting off 6 sts at neck edge every
alt row, twice.

Finish other side of neck, matching shaping.

The '60s

Sweater cont'd

FRONT

With 4mm needles, cast on **80 (86, 94, 100, 112)** sts using M and work 2cm in K1, P1 rib.

Change to 4.5mm needles and cont in st st still using M.

When work measures 34cm from end of ribbing, change to A and cont in st st until work measures 36cm from end of ribbing. Shape armholes by casting off at beg of each row as follows: 4 sts twice, 3 sts twice, 2 sts twice and 1 st twice (4 sts twice, 3 sts twice, 2 sts twice and 1 st 6 times, 4 sts twice, 3 sts 4 times, 2 sts 4 times and 1 st twice, 4 sts twice, 3 sts 4 times, 2 sts 4 times and 1 st 6 times, 5 sts twice, 4 sts twice, 3 sts 4 times, 2 sts 4 times and 1 st 4 times).

60 (62, 64, 66, 70) sts remain.

When work measures **46 (47, 48, 49, 50)** cm from end of ribbing, shape neck by casting off the centre **12 (12, 12, 14, 14)** sts then cont to work one side at a time and cast off at neck edge every alt row as follows: 3 sts twice, 2 sts once, 1 st once then 1 st every 4th row, 4 times.

When work measures **55 (56, 57, 58, 59)** cm from end of ribbing, shape shoulder by casting off at armhole edge every alt row as follows: 2 sts once and 3 sts 3 times (3 sts 4 times; 3 sts 3 times and 4 sts once; 3 sts 3 times and 4 sts once; 3 sts once and 4 sts 3 times).

Finish other side of neck, matching shaping.

SLEEVES

With 4mm needles, cast on **60 (62, 68, 74, 80)** sts using A and work 2cm in K1, P1 rib.

Change to 4.5mm needles and cont in st st still using A.

When work measures 8cm from end of ribbing, shape by casting off at beg of each row as follows: 2 sts 4 times, 1 st 34 times and 2 sts twice (2 sts 4 times, 1 st 32 times and 2 sts 4 times; 2 sts 8 times, 1 st 22 times and 2 sts 8 times; 2 sts 12 times, 1 st 16 times and 2 sts 10 times; 3 sts twice, 2 sts 10 times, 1 st 14 times, 2 sts 10 times and 3 sts twice).

When work measures 23cm from end of ribbing, loosely cast off rem 14 sts. Knit second sleeve to match.

NECKBAND

With 4mm needles, cast on **88 (88, 88, 92, 92)** sts using M and work 2cm in K1, P1 rib. Do one K row on RS and a few rows of st st in another shade. Press these rows, they will be unpicked when attaching neckband.

TO MAKE UP AND FINISH

Join shoulder, side and sleeve seams.

Sew sleeves into armholes.

Sew on the neckband, st by st, using back st, on RS of work.

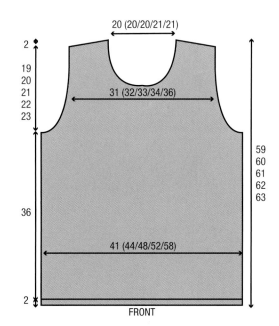

FRONT

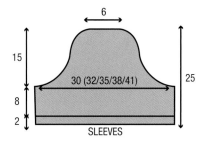

SLEEVES

12 Skirt

SIZES
34-36 (38-40, 42-44, 46-48, 50-52) (see Sizing Charts)

MATERIALS
Aran weight yarn such as Iliade from Phildar (70% acrylic and 30% wool): 3 (3, 3, 3, 3) balls of main colour (M) shown here in Noir; 2 (2, 2, 3, 3) balls of contrast colour (A), shown in Blanc • Pair each 4mm and 4.5mm needles • 15cm zip.

STITCHES USED
K1, P1 rib
Intarsia stranded colourwork using stocking stitch

TENSION
It is essential to check your tension before starting your garment to ensure you get the right measurements.
On 4.5mm needles, 19 sts and 27 rows to 10cm in intarsia stranded colourwork patt worked in st st

INSTRUCTIONS
BACK & FRONT
With 4mm needles, cast on 84 (92, 100, 108, 120) sts in intarsia patt, worked in st st as follows:
21 (23, 25, 27, 30) sts using A, 21 (23, 25, 27, 30) sts using M, rep from * to * once.
When work measures 3cm (8 rows) in tot, mark edge sts with a strand of coloured yarn then change to 4.5mm needles and cont in intarsia patt. Dec 1 in the 3rd st from each end of row, as follows: every 10th row, 7 times and every 8th row, twice.
When work measures 11.5cm from markers, cont in intarsia st st patt as follows:
18 (20, 22, 24, 27) sts using M, 21 (23, 25, 27, 30) sts using A, 21 (23, 25, 27, 30) sts using M and 18 (20, 22, 24, 27) sts using A.
When work measures 23cm from markers, cont as follows:
15 (17, 19, 21, 24) sts using A, 21 (23, 25, 27, 30) sts using M, 21 (23, 25, 27, 30) sts using A and 15 (17, 19, 21, 24) sts using M.
66 (74, 82, 90, 102) sts remain.
When work measures 35cm from markers, change to 4mm needles and cont in K1, P1 rib using M.
When work measures 40cm from markers, cast off loosely in rib.
Knit front in same way.

TO MAKE UP AND FINISH
Join side seams, leaving a 15cm opening on one side for the zip. Make a hem along the bottom edge of the skirt and stitch on the inside using sewing thread and concealed stitching. Sew zip to side seam opening.

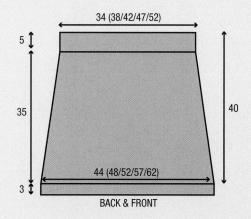

34 (38/42/47/52)

5

35

40

44 (48/52/57/62)

3

BACK & FRONT

13 Dress

Stocking stitch with ribbed edging.
Sport weight such as Partner 3.5.
Can be lengthened.

14 Coat

Stocking stitch with ribbed edging.
Chunky yarn such as Nébuleuse.

13 Dress

SIZES
34-36 (38-40, 42-44, 46-48, 50-52) (see Sizing Charts)

MATERIALS
5-ply or Sport weight yarn such as Partner 3.5 from Phildar (50% polyamide, 25% worsted wool and 25% acrylic): **8 (9, 10, 11, 12)** balls of main colour (M), shown here in Écru; **1 (1, 1, 1, 1)** ball of 1st contrast colour (A), shown in Orge; **1 (1, 1, 1, 1)** ball of 2nd contrast colour (B), shown in Fuchsia; **1 (1, 1, 1, 1)** ball of 3rd contrast colour (C), shown in Vermillon • Pair each 3mm and 3.5mm needles • 5 Buttons

STITCHES USED
K1, P1 rib
Stocking stitch

TENSION
It is essential to check your tension before starting your garment to ensure you get the right measurements.
On 3.5mm needles, 24 sts and 30 rows to 10cm in st st.

INSTRUCTIONS
BACK
With 3mm needles, cast on **110 (118, 128, 136, 152)** sts using B and work 5cm in K1, P1 rib then do 1 row P on WS.
Change to 3.5mm needles and cont in st st using M. Dec 1 in the 3rd st from each end of every foll 32nd row, 5 times.
100 (108, 118, 126, 142) sts remain.
When work measures 63cm from end of ribbing, shape armholes by casting off at beg of each row as follows:
34-36: 4 sts twice, 3 sts twice, 2 sts 4 times and 1 st twice
38-40: 4 sts twice, 3 sts 4 times, 2 sts 4 times and 1 st twice
42-44: 4 sts twice, 3 sts 4 times, 2 sts 6 times and 1 st 4 times
46-48: 5 sts twice, 4 sts twice, 3 sts 4 times, 2 sts 4 times and 1 st 4 times
50-52: 5 sts twice, 4 sts 4 times, 3 sts 4 times, 2 sts 6 times and 1 st 4 times
76 (78, 82, 84, 88) sts remain.
When work measures **82 (83, 84, 85, 86)** cm from end of ribbing, shape shoulders by casting off at beg of every alt row at outside edge as follows: 4 sts 4 times (4 sts 3 times and 5 sts once; 4 sts once and 5 sts 3 times; 4 sts once and 5 sts 3 times; 5 sts 3 times and 6 sts once).
At the same time, shape neck by casting off the centre **16 (16, 16, 18, 18)** sts and working one side at a time cast off 7 sts at neck edge every alt row, twice. Finish other side of neck.

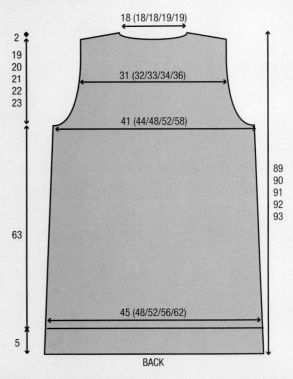

BACK

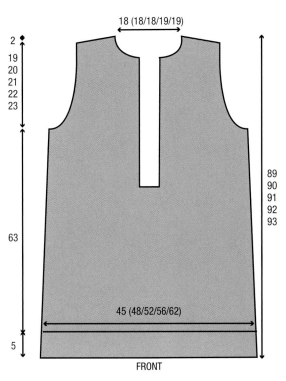

FRONT

FRONT

With 3mm needles, cast on **110 (118, 128, 136, 152)** sts using B and work 5cm in K1, P1 rib then do 1 row P on WS.

Change to 3.5mm needles and cont in st st using M. Dec 1 in the 3rd st from each end of every foll 32nd row, 5 times.

100 (108, 118, 126, 142) sts remain.

When work measures **44 (45, 46, 47, 48)** cm from end of ribbing, cast off centre 10 sts then cont, working one side at a time.

When work measures 63cm from end of ribbing, shape armhole by casting off at outside edge every alt row:

34-36: 4 sts once, 3 sts once, 2 sts twice and 1 st once

38-40: 4 sts once, 3 sts twice, 2 sts twice and 1 st once

42-44: 4 sts once, 3 sts twice, 2 sts 3 times and 1 st twice

46-48: 5 sts once, 4 sts once, 3 sts twice, 2 sts twice and 1 st twice

50-52: 5 sts once, 4 sts twice, 3 sts twice, 2 sts 3 times and 1 st twice

When work measures **78 (79, 80, 81, 82)** cm from end of ribbing, shape neck by casting off at front opening edge every alt row as follows

34-36: 4 sts once, 3 sts twice, 2 sts twice and 1 st 3 times

38-40: 4 sts once, 3 sts twice, 2 sts twice and 1 st 3 times

42-44: 4 sts once, 3 sts twice, 2 sts twice and 1 st 3 times

46-48: 4 sts twice, 3 sts twice, 2 sts twice and 1 st twice

50-52: 4 sts once, 3 sts twice, 2 sts twice and 1 st 3 times

When work measures **82 (83, 84, 85, 86)** cm from end of ribbing, shape shoulder by casting off at armhole edge every alt row as follows: 4 sts 4 times (4 sts 3 times and 5 sts once; 4 sts once and 5 sts 3 times; 4 sts once and 5 sts 3 times; 5 sts 3 times and 6 sts once).

Finish other side of neck, matching shaping.

Dress cont'd

SLEEVES

With 3mm needles, cast on **64 (70, 74, 78, 84)** sts using A and work 5cm in K1, P1 rib then do 1 P row on WS.

Change to 3.5mm needles and cont in st st using M. Inc 1 in the 3rd st from each end of row as follows: every 16th row, 3 times and every 14th row, twice (every 18th row 4 times; every 14th row 3 times and every 12th row 3 times; every 10th row 8 times; every 10th row 8 times). **74 (78, 86, 94, 100)** sts.

When work measures 30cm from end of ribbing, shape by casting off at beg of each row as follows:

34-36: 2 sts 8 times, 1 st 14 times, work 2 rows straight then 1 st 16 times and 2 sts 6 times

38-40: 2 sts 10 times, 1 st 12 times, work 2 rows straight then 1 st 14 times and 2 sts 8 times

42-44: 3 sts twice, 2 sts 10 times, 1 st 10 times, work 2 rows straight then 1 st 12 times, 2 sts 8 times and 3 sts twice

46-48: 3 sts 4 times, 2 sts 10 times, 1 st 8 times, work 2 rows straight then 1 st 10 times, 2 sts 8 times and 3 sts 4 times

50-52: 3 sts 4 times, 2 sts 12 times, 1 st 6 times, work 2 rows straight then 1 st 6 times, 2 sts 12 times and 3 sts 4 times

When work measures 45cm from end of ribbing, loosely cast off rem 16 sts. Knit second sleeve to match.

COLLAR

With 3mm needles, cast on **109 (109, 109, 113, 113)** sts using C. Work 3cm in K1, P1 rib, starting and ending first row and every odd row (RS) with K2 then do 1 row K on RS and a few rows of st st in another shade.

Press these rows, they will be unpicked when assembling the dress.

BUTTONBAND

With 3mm needles cast on 89 sts using C. Work 3cm in K1, P1 rib, starting and ending first row and every odd row (RS) with K2 then do 1 row K on RS and a few rows of st st in another shade.

Press these rows, they will be unpicked when assembling the dress.

Knit buttonhole band in same way but making 5 buttonholes over 2 sts on the 6th row, with first buttonhole positioned 4 sts from edge and others evenly spaced, 18 sts apart.

TO MAKE UP AND FINISH

Join shoulder, side and sleeve seams. Sew sleeves into armholes. Sew collar to neckline, st by st, using back st, on RS of work. Sew buttonband and buttonhole band to front opening edges and edge of collar, st by st, using back st on RS of work. Sew on buttons.

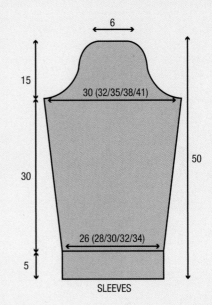

SLEEVES

14 Coat

SIZES

34-36 (38-40, 42-44, 46-48, 50-52) (see Sizing Charts)

MATERIALS

Chunky yarn such as Nébuleuse from Phildar (41% wool, 41% acrylic and 18% polyamide): **12 (12, 13, 15, 16)** balls of main colour (M), shown here in Tomette shade; **3 (3, 3, 3, 4)** balls of 1st contrast colour (A), shown in Blush, **3 (3, 3, 4, 4)** balls of 2nd contrast colour (B), shown here in Biche • Pair each 6mm and 7mm needles • 5 buttons for covering • 5 press studs

STITCHES USED

K1, P1 rib
Stocking stitch

TENSION

It is essential to check your tension before starting your garment to ensure you get the right measurements.
On 7mm needles, 23 sts and 37 rows to 20cm in st st.

INSTRUCTIONS

BACK

With 7mm needles cast on **56 (60, 64, 68, 76)** sts using B and work 20cm in st st then switch to A and cont in st st until work measures 27cm in tot. Switch to M and cont in st st.
When work measures 65cm in tot, mark edge sts with a strand of coloured yarn to mark armholes.
When work measures **87 (88, 89, 90, 91)** cm in tot, shape shoulders by casting off at beg of every alt row at outside edge as follows: 5 sts once and 6 sts twice (6 sts twice and 7 sts once; 7 sts 3 times; 7 sts twice and 8 sts once; 8 sts once and 9 sts twice).
At the same time, shape neck by casting off the centre **10 (10, 10, 12, 12)** sts and cont, working one side at a time, casting off 6 sts at neck edge on foll alt row, once.
Finish other side of neck, matching shaping.

RIGHT FRONT

With 7mm needles cast on **34 (36, 38, 40, 44)** sts using B and work 20cm in st st then switch to A and cont in st st until work measures 27cm in tot. Switch to M and cont in st st.
When work measures 65cm in tot, mark LH edge st with a strand of coloured yarn to mark armhole.
When work measures **80 (81, 82, 83, 84)** cm in tot, mark 8th st with a strand of coloured yarn then shape neck by casting off **9 (9, 9, 10, 10)** sts at RH edge.
Cont to cast off at RH edge on every alt row as follows on all sizes: 3 sts once, 2 sts once and 1 st twice, then 1 st on foll 4th row, once.
When work measures **87 (88, 89, 90, 91)** cm in tot, shape shoulder by casting off at LH edge every alt row: 5 sts once and 6 sts twice (6 sts twice and 7 sts once; 7 sts 3 times; 7 sts twice and 8 sts once; 8 sts once and 9 sts twice).
Make left front, reversing shaping.

SLEEVES

With 7mm needles cast on **34 (36, 38, 42, 44)** sts using M and work in st st.
Inc 1 in the 3rd st from each end of row, as follows:
34-36: every 8th row 4 times and every 6th row 5 times
38-40: every 8th row 3 times and every 6th row 6 times
42-44: every 8th row twice and every 6th row 7 times
46-48: every 8th row 4 times and every 6th row 4 times
50-52: every 8th row 3 times and every 6th row 5 times
52 (54, 56, 58, 60) sts.
When work measures **36.5 (36, 35, 34, 32)** cm in tot, cast off loosely.
Knit second sleeve to match.

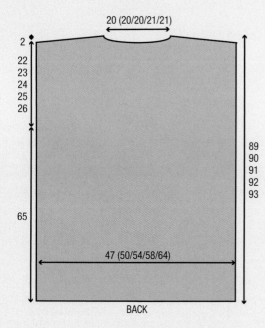

20 (20/20/21/21)

2
22
23
24
25
26

89
90
91
92
93

65

47 (50/54/58/64)

BACK

COLLAR

With 6mm needles, cast on **75 (75, 75, 79, 79)** sts using A and work 10cm in K1, P1 rib, starting and ending first row and every odd row (RS) with K2 then cast off 6 sts at beg of next 6 rows.
Cast off rem sts on foll alt row.

TO MAKE UP AND FINISH

Join shoulder seams. Fit sleeves in armholes, between coloured markers. Join side and sleeve seams. Sew collar around neckline, aligning ends of collar with coloured markers. Cover 4 buttons using M and 1 button using A. Sew on press studs, evenly spaced apart. Sew buttons over press studs.

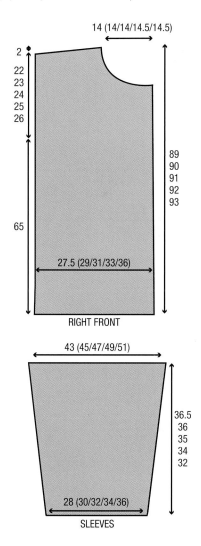

14 (14/14/14.5/14.5)

2
22
23
24
25
26

89
90
91
92
93

65

27.5 (29/31/33/36)

RIGHT FRONT

43 (45/47/49/51)

36.5
36
35
34
32

28 (30/32/34/36)

SLEEVES

15 Jacket

Stocking stitch with ribbed edging.
Aran weight yarn such as Quiétude.

16 Sweater

3/4 sleeves with cable pattern and wide ribbing with narrow ribbed edging. Aran weight yarn such as Iliade.

15 Jacket

SIZES

34-36 (38-40, 42-44, 46-48, 50-52) (see Sizing Charts)

MATERIALS

Aran weight yarn such as Quiétude from Phildar (50% worsted wool and 50% acrylic): **10 (11, 12, 13, 14)** balls, shown here in Violet • Pair each 3.5mm and 4mm needles • 3mm crochet hook • 1 belt buckle • 1 x 50cm zip

STITCHES USED

K1, P1 rib
Stocking stitch

TENSION

It is essential to check your tension before starting your garment to ensure you get the right measurements.
On 4mm needles, 32 sts and 53 rows to 20cm in st st.

INSTRUCTIONS
BACK

With 3.5mm needles, cast on **74 (78, 86, 92, 102)** sts and work 3cm (8 rows) in st st then mark edge stitches with a strand of coloured yarn to denote hem. Change to 4mm needles and cont in st st. Dec 1 in 3rd st from each end of row, as follows: every 14th row 4 times and foll 12th row once (every 16th row 4 times; every 14th row 4 times and foll 12th row once; every 16th row 4 times; every 14th row 4 times and foll 12th row once). **64 (70, 76, 84, 92)** sts remain.

When work measures 30cm from coloured markers, inc 1 in 3rd st from each end of next row then rep as follows: foll 24th row once (cont straight for all other sizes.) **68 (72, 78, 86, 94)** sts.

When work measures 48cm from coloured markers, shape raglan by dec **1 (1, 1, 2, 2)** sts at each end then cast off at beg of each row as follows:

34-36: 1 st 42 times, work 2 rows straight then 1 st twice

38-40: *1 st 14 times, work 2 rows straight, then 1 st twice* rep from * to * once, then 1 st 16 times

42-44: 1 st 54 times

46-48: 1 st 28 times, 2 sts twice, 1 st 26 times

50-52: *1 st 10 times, 2 sts twice*, rep from * to * 3 more times then 1 st 10 times.

When work measures **67 (68, 69, 70, 71)** cm from coloured markers, cast off rem **22 (22, 22, 24, 24)** sts loosely.

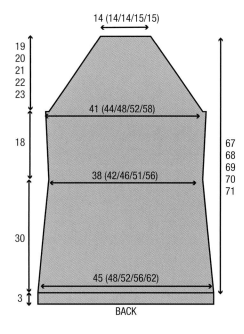

14 (14/14/15/15)

19
20
21
22
23

41 (44/48/52/58)

18

38 (42/46/51/56)

67
68
69
70
71

30

45 (48/52/56/62)

3

BACK

RIGHT FRONT

With 3.5mm needles, cast on **37 (39, 43, 46, 51)** sts and work 3cm (8 rows) in st st then mark edge stitches with a strand of coloured yarn to denote hem. Change to 4mm needles and cont in st st. Dec 1 in 3rd st from LH edge as follows: every 14th row 4 times and foll 12th row once (every 16th row 4 times; every 14th row 4 times and foll 12th row once; every 16th row 4 times; every 14th row 4 times and foll 12th row once). **32 (35, 38, 42, 46)** sts remain. When work measures 30cm from coloured markers, inc 1 in 3rd st from LH edge in next row then rep as follows: foll 24th row once **(cont straight for all other sizes)**. **34 (36, 39, 43, 47)** sts.

When work measures 48cm from coloured markers, shape raglan by casting off **1 (1, 1, 2, 2)** sts at LH edge on next row then rep as follows:

34-36: 1 st every alt row 20 times **(13 sts)**

38-40: *1 st every alt row 7 times then 1 st foll 4th row once,* rep from * to * 2 times in tot and then 1 st every alt row 4 times

42-44: 1 st every alt row, 22 times

46-48: every alt row: 1 st 14 times, 2 sts once and 1 st 9 times

50-52: every alt row: *1 st 5 times, 2 sts once*, rep from * to *4 times in tot and finish with 1 st every alt row, twice

When work measures **60 (61, 62, 63, 64)** cm from coloured markers, shape neck by casting off at RH edge every alt row as follows:

34-36: 4 sts once, 3 sts once, 2 sts once, 1 st twice and 2 sts once

38-40: 4 sts once, 3 sts once, 2 sts 4 times

42-44: 4 sts once, 3 sts once, 2 sts once, 1 st twice and 2 sts once

46-48: 4 sts once, 3 sts twice and 2 sts 3 times

50-52: 4 sts once, 3 sts once, 2 sts 4 times

Make left front, reversing shaping.

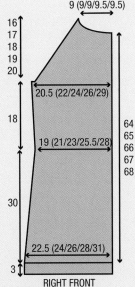

RIGHT FRONT

Jacket cont'd

RIGHT SLEEVE

With 3.5mm needles, cast on **40 (44, 46, 50, 54)** sts and work 3cm in K1, P1 rib.

Change to 4mm needles and cont in st st. Inc 1 in 3rd st from each end of row, as follows: every 24th row, twice and every 22nd row, twice (every 20th row 3 times and every 18th row twice; foll 16th row once and every 14th row 6 times; every 14th row 3 times and every 12th row 5 times; every 10th row 9 times and every 8th row twice). **48 (54, 60, 66, 76)** sts.

When work measures 43cm from end of ribbing, shape raglan by dec 1 (1, 1, 2, 2) sts at each end and then cast off at beg of each row as follows:

34-36: 1 st 40 times

38-40: *1 st 14 times, work 2 rows straight, then 1 st twice* rep from * to * and then 1 st 8 times (40 sts)

42-44: 1 st 44 times

46-48: 1 st 28 times, 2 sts twice, 1 st 18 times (50 sts)

50-52: *1 st 10 times, 2 sts twice*, rep from * to * 3 more times in tot and then 1 st 4 times (60 sts)

When work measures **59 (60, 61, 62, 63)** cm from end of ribbing, cast off at RH edge every alt row as follows:

34-36: 1 st once, then every 4th row, 1 st once and 2 sts once

38-40: 2 sts twice, 1 st twice and 2 sts once

42-44: 3 sts twice, 2 sts once, 1 st twice and 2 sts once

46-48: 2 sts twice, 1 st twice and 2 sts once

50-52: 3 sts once and 2 sts 3 times

At the same time, cast off at LH edge as follows:

34-36: 1 st once then 1 st on foll 4th row once

38-40: 1 st once then 1 st every alt row, 3 times

42-44: 1 st on foll 4th row, once, then 1 st on foll 4th row, once

46-48: 1 st once then 1 st every alt row, 3 times

50-52: 1 st once then 1 st every alt row, twice

Make left sleeve, reversing shaping.

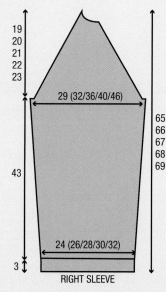

29 (32/36/40/46)

19
20
21
22
23

65
66
67
68
69

43

24 (26/28/30/32)

3

RIGHT SLEEVE

COLLAR

With 3.5mm needles, cast on **102 (102, 102, 104, 104)** sts and work in K1, P1 rib, starting and ending first row and every odd row (RS) with K2. Work short rows, leaving stitches unworked or on holder each end on alt rows as follows: 3 sts 4 times and 4 sts 3 times then work one row across all sts.

Work 1 row of K on RS then a few rows of st st in another shade. Press these rows, they will be unpicked when attaching collar to jacket.

BELT

With 3.5mm needles, cast on 13 sts and work **106 (110, 114, 119, 124)** cm in K1, P1 rib then cast off loosely.

TO MAKE UP AND FINISH

Match raglan edges of sleeves to body with shorter side at the front. Join side and sleeve seams. Sew on collar, st by st, using back st, on RS of work. Make hem and stitch on inside using sewing thread with concealed stitching. Stitch on the zip, starting at top of neck. With 3mm crochet hook, crochet 2 x 5cm lengths of chain stitch to make belt loops at side seams, 20cm below armholes. Fold 2cm of belt over buckle and attach with concealed stitching.

16 Sweater

SIZES
34-36 (38-40, 42-44, 46-48, 50-52) (see Sizing Charts)

MATERIALS
An Aran weight yarn such as Iliade from Phildar (70% acrylic and 30% wool):
10 (11, 11, 12, 14) balls, shown here in Fraise shade • Pair of 4.5mm needles
• 3mm crochet hook • 2 cable needles • 1 belt buckle

STITCHES USED
K1, P1 rib
K3, P3 rib
Cable pattern stitch: see chart and legends

TENSION
It is essential to check your tension before starting your garment to ensure you get the right measurements.
On 4.5mm needles, 20 sts and 27 rows to 10cm in K3, P3 rib (tension counted when stretched widthways)
On 4.5mm needles, 10 sts in patt = 4cm

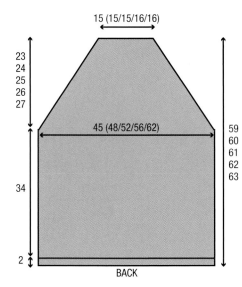

INSTRUCTIONS
BACK
With 4.5mm needles, cast on **92 (98, 104, 110, 122)** sts and work 2cm in K1, P1 rib.
Now continue in K3, P3 rib. Inc 1 on first row, starting and ending first row and every odd row (RS) with P3 (K3, P3, K3, K3).
93 (99, 105, 111, 123) sts.
When work measures 36cm in tot, shape raglan by casting off 2 sts at beg of foll 2 rows. Cont by casting off at beg of each row as follows:
34-36: 1 st 58 times
38-40: 1 st 30 times, 2 sts twice and 1 st 30 times
42-44: *1 st 20 times, 2 sts twice*, rep from * to * and finish with 1 st 22 times
46-48: *1 st 16 times, 2 sts twice*, rep from * to * twice more and finish with 1 st 14 times (33 times)
50-52: *1 st 6 times, 2 sts twice*, rep from * to * 7 more times and finish with 1 st 6 times
When work measures **59 (60, 61, 62, 63)** cm in tot, cast off rem **31 (31, 31, 33, 33)** sts.

FRONT
With 4.5mm needles, cast on **92 (98, 104, 110, 122)** sts and work 2cm in K1, P1 rib.
Now cont in K3, P3 rib and patt. Inc 3 on first row and set patt as follows:
27 (30, 33, 36, 42) sts in K3, P3 rib starting with P3 (K3, P3, K3, K3) and ending with P3, work 10 sts of panel patt (see chart), 21 sts in K3, P3 rib, starting and ending with P3, work 10 sts of panel patt (see chart) and **27 (30, 33, 36, 42)** sts of K3, P3 rib starting with P3 and ending with P3 (K3, P3, K3, K3).
95 (101, 107, 113, 125) sts.
When work measures 36cm in tot, shape raglan by casting off 2 sts at beg of foll 2 rows, then cont by casting off at beg of each row as follows:
34-36: 1 st 58 times **(33 sts remain)**
38-40: 1 st 30 times, 2 sts twice and 1 st 22 times **(41 sts remain)**
42-44: *1 st 20 times, 2 sts twice*, rep from * to * and finish with 1 st 14 times **(45 sts remain)**
46-48: *1 st 16 times, 2 sts twice*, rep from * to * twice more and finish with 1 st 6 times **(43 sts remain)**
50-52: *1 st 6 times, 2 sts twice*, rep from * to * 6 more times and finish with 1 st 6 times **(45 sts remain)**
When work measures **49 (50, 51, 52, 53)** cm in tot, shape neck by casting off the centre **15 (15, 15, 17, 17)** sts then cont, working on one side at a time and cast off at neck edge every alt row as follows:
34-36: 3 sts once, 2 sts once and 1 st 6 times, then on foll 4th row, 2 sts once
38-40: 3 sts once, 2 sts twice, 1 st 5 times, then on foll 4th row 2 sts once
42-44: 3 sts once, 2 sts twice, 1 st 5 times then on foll 4th row 2 sts once
46-48: 3 sts once, 2 sts twice, 1 st 5 times then on foll 4th row 2 sts once
50-52: 3 sts once, 2 sts 3 times, 1 st 4 times then on foll 4th row 2 sts once
Finish other side of neck.

Sweater cont'd

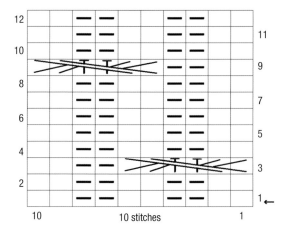

| K on RS; P on WS. |
| – P on RS; K on WS. |

>⨯⨯⨯< 6 left-crossed sts: slip next 2 sts onto first cable needle (CN1) leave at front of work, slip next 2 sts onto 2nd CN (CN2) leave at back of work, K2 from LHN, P2 from CN2 and K2 from CN1.

RIGHT SLEEVE

With 4.5mm needles, cast on **50 (56, 56, 62, 68)** sts and work 2cm in K1, P1 rib.

Now cont in K3, P3 rib. Inc 1 on first row, starting and ending first row and every odd row (RS) with K3.

51 (57, 57, 63, 69) sts.

Inc 1 at each end of row as follows:

34-36: every 10th row twice and every 8th row 6 times

38-40: every 8th row 7 times and on foll 6th row once

42-44: every 6th row 8 times and every 4th row 4 times

46-48: every 6th row 6 times and every 4th row 7 times

50-52: every 4th row 16 times

67 (73, 81, 89, 101) sts.

When work measures 27cm in tot, shape raglan by casting off 2 sts at beg of foll 2 rows then cont casting off at beg of each row as follows:

34-36: 1 st 52 times **(11 sts remain)**

38-40: 1 st 30 times, 2 sts twice and 1 st 22 times **(17 sts remain)**

42-44: *1 st 20 times, 2 sts twice*, rep from * to * once more and finish with 1 st 14 times **(19 sts remain)**

46-48: *1 st 16 times, 2 sts twice*, rep from * to * twice more and finish with 1 st 6 times **(19 sts remain)**

50-52: *1 st 6 times, 2 sts twice*, rep from * to * six more times and finish with 1 st 6 times **(21 sts remain)**

When work measures **47 (48, 49, 50, 51)** cm in tot, cont casting off at RH edge every alt row:

34-36: 2 sts twice, 1 st twice and 2 sts once

38-40: 3 sts once, 2 sts once, 1 st twice and 2 sts once

42-44: 3 sts twice, 2 sts once, 1 st once and 2 sts once

46-48: 4 sts once, 3 sts 3 times and 2 sts once

50-52: 4 sts twice, 3 sts twice and 2 sts once

At the same time, cast off at LH edge: 1 st once then 1 st every alt row, twice (1 st once then 1 st every alt row, 3 times; 1 st once then 1 st every alt row 3 times; 1 st once then 1 st every alt row 3 times; 2 sts once then 1 st every alt row 3 times).

Make left sleeve, reversing shaping.

NECKBAND

With 4.5mm needles, cast on **114 (114, 114, 118, 118)** sts and work 2cm in K1, P1 rib then work a P row on WS and a few rows of st st in another shade. Press these rows, they will be unpicked when attaching the neckband.

BELT

With 4.5mm needles, cast on 9 sts and work **106 (110, 114, 119, 123)** cm in K1, P1 rib then cast off loosely.

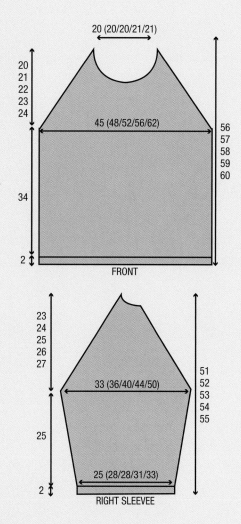

FRONT

RIGHT SLEEVEE

TO MAKE UP AND FINISH

Match sleeves' raglan edges to body (shorter side goes to the front). Join side and sleeve seams. Sew on the neckband, st by st, using back st, on RS of work. Fold 2cm of belt over buckle and attach with concealed stitching. With a 3mm crochet hook, make a 5cm chain to form a belt loop on side seam, 14cm below armhole. Do same on other side. Slip belt through loops.

17 Dress

K3, P3 rib and K6, P6 rib.
Aran weight yarn such
as Frimas.

17 Dress

SIZES
34-36 (38-40, 42-44, 46-48, 50-52) (see Sizing Charts)

MATERIALS
Aran weight yarn such as Frimas from Phildar (50% wool and 50% cotton): **12 (13, 14, 15, 17)** balls, shown here in Corail shade • Pair 6mm needles

STITCHES USED
K3, P3 rib
K6, P6 rib

TENSION
It is essential to check your tension before starting your garment to ensure you get the right measurements.
On 6mm needles, 31 sts and 43 rows to 20cm in K6, P6 rib

INSTRUCTIONS
BACK
With 6mm needles, cast on **68 (74, 80, 86, 98)** sts and work 20cm in K3, P3 rib, starting first row and every odd row (RS) with K3 and ending with K2.
Cont in K6, P6 rib, starting and ending first row and every odd row (RS) with P7 (K4, P7, K4, K4).
When work measures 58cm in tot, shape armholes by casting off at beg of each row as follows: 3 sts twice, 2 sts 4 times and 1 st twice (3 sts 4 times, 2 sts twice and 1 st 4 times; 4 sts twice, 3 sts twice, 2 sts twice and 1 st 6 times; 4 sts twice, 3 sts 4 times, 2 sts twice and 1 st 4 times; 4 sts twice, 3 sts 4 times, 2 sts 6 times and 1 st 6 times).
52 (54, 56, 58, 60) sts remain.
When work measures **77 (78, 79, 80, 81)** cm in tot, shape shoulders by casting off at beg of every alt row at outside edge as follows: 3 sts once and 4 sts twice (4 sts 3 times; 4 sts twice and 5 sts once; 4 sts twice and 5 sts once; 5 sts twice and 4 sts once).
At the same time, shape neck by casting off the centre **14 (14, 14, 16, 16)** sts and cont, working one side at a time, casting off 8 sts at neck edge on foll alt row.
Finish other side of neck.

FRONT
With 6mm needles, cast on **68 (74, 80, 86, 98)** sts and work 20cm in K3, P3 rib, starting first row and every odd row (RS) with K3 and ending with K2.
Cont in K6, P6 rib, starting and ending first row and every odd row (RS) with P7 (K4, P7, K4, K4).
When work measures 58cm in tot, shape armholes by casting off at beg of each row as follows: 3 sts twice, 2 sts 4 times and 1 st twice (3 sts 4 times, 2 sts twice and 1 st 4 times; 4 sts twice, 3 sts twice, 2 sts twice and 1 st 6 times; 4 sts twice, 3 sts 4 times, 2 sts twice and 1 st 4 times; 4 sts twice, 3 sts 4 times, 2 sts 6 times and 1 st 6 times).
52 (54, 56, 58, 60) sts remain.
When work measures **69 (70, 71, 72, 73)** cm in tot, shape neck by casting off the centre **10 (10, 10, 12, 12)** sts then cont to work one side at a time, casting off at neck edge every alt row as follows: 3 sts once, 2 sts once, 1 st 3 times, then 1 st every 4th row, twice.
When work measures **77 (78, 79, 80, 81)** cm in tot, shape shoulder by casting off at armhole edge every alt row: 3 sts once and 4 sts twice (4 sts 3 times; 4 sts twice and 5 sts once; 4 sts twice and 5 sts once; 5 sts twice and 4 sts once).
Finish other side of neck.

SLEEVES
With 6mm needles, cast on **38 (38, 44, 44, 50)** sts and work 10cm in K3, P3 rib, starting first row and every odd row (RS) with K3 and ending with K2.
Cont in K6, P6 rib. Inc **10 (14, 10, 14, 10)** sts evenly on first row, starting and

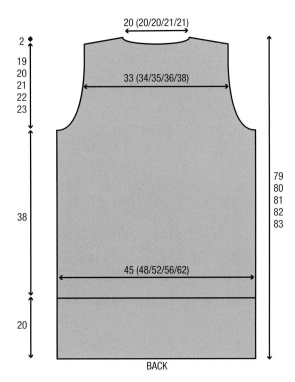

20 (20/20/21/21)

2
19
20
21
22
23

33 (34/35/36/38)

79
80
81
82
83

38

45 (48/52/56/62)

20

BACK

ending first row and every odd row (RS) with K3 (K5, K6, K2, K3).
48 (52, 54, 58, 60) sts.
When work measures 45cm in tot, shape by casting off at beg of each row as follows:
34-36: 2 sts twice, 1 st 14 times, work 2 rows straight, then 1 st 12 times and 2 sts twice
38-40: 2 sts 4 times, 1 st 10 times, work 2 rows straight then 1 st 12 times and 2 sts 4 times
42-44: 2 sts 4 times, 1 st 24 times and 2 sts 4 times
46-48: 2 sts 6 times, 1 st 20 times and 2 sts 6 times
50-52: 2 sts 8 times, 1 st 18 times and 2 sts 6 times
When work measures 60cm, loosely cast off rem 14 sts.
Knit second sleeve to match.

COLLAR

With 6mm needles, cast on **92 (92, 92, 98, 98)** sts and work 25cm in K3, P3 rib, starting first row and every odd row (RS) with K3 and ending with K2, then do 1 row P on WS and a few rows of st st in another shade. Press these rows, they will be unpicked when attaching the collar.

TO MAKE UP AND FINISH

Join shoulder, side and sleeve seams. Sew sleeves into armholes. Join ends of collar, with half the seam on one side of work and half on other side for the turn down section. Sew collar to neckline, st by st, using back stitch on RS.

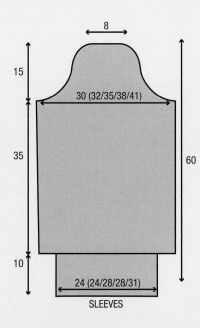

8

15

30 (32/35/38/41)

35

60

10

24 (24/28/28/31)

SLEEVES

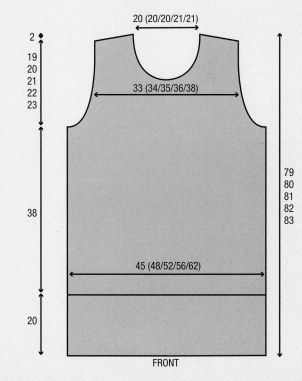

20 (20/20/21/21)

2

19
20
21
22
23

33 (34/35/36/38)

38

79
80
81
82
83

45 (48/52/56/62)

20

FRONT

18 Cardigan Jacket

Stocking stitch with ribbed edging.
Double knitting such as Laine & Coton.

19 Sweater

Stocking stitch stripes with ribbed edging.
Double knitting such as Laine & Coton.

18 Cardigan Jacket

SIZES
S (15-17 yrs), M (42-44), L (46-48), XL (50-52), XXL (54-56) (see Sizing Charts) S (M, L, XL, XXL)

MATERIALS
Double knitting such as Laine & Coton from Phildar (50% wool and 50% cotton): **10 (10, 11, 12, 13)** balls of main colour (M), shown here in Denim shade; **2 (2, 2, 2, 2)** balls of contrast colour (A), shown in Sable • Pair each 3mm and 3.5mm needles • 6 Buttons

STITCHES USED
K1, P1 rib
Stocking stitch

TENSION
It is essential to check your tension before starting your garment to ensure you get the right measurements.
On 3.5mm needles, 20 sts and 29 rows to 10cm in st st.

INSTRUCTIONS
BACK
With 3mm needles, cast on **93 (99, 107, 115, 123)** sts using A and work 2cm in K1, P1 rib then do 1 row P on WS using A.
Change to 3.5mm needles and cont in st st using M. Inc by 1 st on first row.
94 (100, 108, 116, 124) sts.
When work measures 43cm from end of ribbing, shape armholes by casting off at beg of each row as follows: 3 sts twice, 2 sts twice and 1 st 4 times (3 sts twice, 2 sts 4 times and 1 st twice, 3 sts twice, 2 sts 4 times and 1 st 6 times, 3 sts 4 times, 2 sts 4 times and 1 st twice, 3 sts 4 times, 2 sts 4 times and 1 st 4 times).
80 (84, 88, 94, 100) sts remain.
When work measures **64 (65, 66, 67, 68)** cm from end of ribbing, shape shoulders by casting off at beg of every alt row at outside edge as follows: 4 sts once and 5 sts 3 times (5 sts 4 times, 5 sts twice and 6 sts twice, 6 sts 4 times, 6 sts once and 7 sts 3 times).
At the same time, shape neck by casting off the centre **12 (14, 14, 16, 16)** sts and cont, working one side at a time, casting off at neck edge every alt row: 7 sts once and 8 sts once.
Finish other side of neck.

RIGHT FRONT
With 3mm needles, cast on **45 (49, 53, 57, 61)** sts using A and work 2cm in K1, P1 rib, starting first row and every odd row (RS) with K2, then do 1 row P on WS using A.
Change to 3.5mm needles and cont in st st using M.
When work measures **39 (40, 41, 42, 43)** cm from end of ribbing, shape neck by casting off 1 st at RH edge and then rep as follows: every 4th row, 18 times, every alt row, 3 times and every 4th row, 17 times, every alt row, 3 times and every 4th row, 17 times, every alt row, 5 times and every 4th row, 16 times, every alt row, 5 times and every 4th row, 16 times).
Meanwhile, when work measures 43cm from end of ribbing, shape armhole by casting off at LH edge every alt row: 3 sts once, 2 sts once and 1 st twice (3 sts once, 2 sts twice and 1 st once, 3 sts once, 2 sts twice and 1 st 3 times, 3 sts twice, 2 sts twice and 1 st once, 3 sts twice, 2 sts twice and 1 st twice).
When work measures **64 (65, 66, 67, 68)** cm from end of ribbing, shape shoulder by casting off at armhole edge every alt row as follows: 4 sts once and 5 sts 3 times (5 sts 4 times, 5 sts twice and 6 sts twice, 6 sts 4 times, 6 sts once and 7 sts 3 times).
Make left front, reversing shaping.

SLEEVES
With 3mm needles, cast on **50 (54, 58, 62, 66)** sts using A and work 2cm in K1, P1 rib then do 1 P row on WS using A.
Change to 3.5mm needles and cont in st st using M. Inc 1 in the 3rd st from each end of every 14th row, 5 times and every 12th row, 5 times.
70 (74, 78, 82, 86) sts.
When work measures 49cm in tot, shape by casting off at beg of each row as follows:
2 sts 6 times, 1 st 14 times, work 2 rows straight then 1 st 16 times and 2 sts 6 times (2 sts 8 times, 1 st 12 times, work 2 rows straight then 1 st 14 times and 2 sts 8 times, 3 sts twice, 2 sts 6 times, 1 st 12 times, work 2 rows straight then 1 st 14 times, 2 sts 6 times and 3 sts twice, 3 sts twice, 2 sts 8 times, 1 st 10 times, work 2 rows straight then 1 st 12 times, 2 sts 8 times and 3 sts twice, 3 sts twice, 2 sts 10 times, 1 st 8 times, work 2 rows straight then 1 st 10 times, 2 sts 10 times and 3 sts twice).
Cont until work measures 64cm from end of ribbing then loosely cast off rem 16 sts.
Knit second sleeve to match.

BUTTON & BUTTONHOLE BAND
With 3mm needles, cast on 9 sts using A. Work in K1, P1 rib, starting and ending first row and every odd row (RS) with K2.
Make 6 buttonholes over 3 rows, the first at 1cm from start of work and the others spaced **6.5 (6.5, 7, 7, 7)** cm apart.
When work measures **157 (160, 162, 165, 167)** cm in tot, cast off loosely in rib.

FALSE POCKETS
With 3.5mm needles, cast on 27 sts using A and work 2cm in K1, P1 rib, starting and ending first row and every odd row (RS) with K2 then do 1 row K on RS and a few rows of st st in another shade.
Press these rows, they will be unpicked when attaching pockets to jacket.
Knit second false pocket to match.

TO MAKE UP AND FINISH

Join shoulder, side and sleeve seams. Sew sleeves into armholes. Sew button and buttonhole band along front edges and back of neck. Sew false pockets to front, 15cm up from bottom and 5cm from buttonhole, buttonband edge, st by st, using back stitch on RS of work.

Sew on buttons.

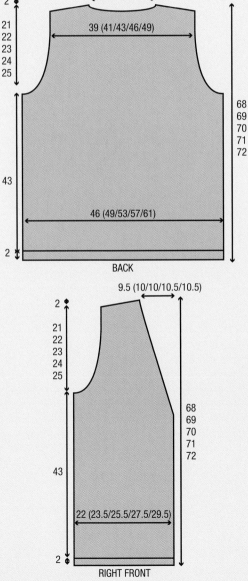

21 (22/22/23/23)

2

21
22
23
24
25

39 (41/43/46/49)

68
69
70
71
72

43

46 (49/53/57/61)

2

BACK

9.5 (10/10/10.5/10.5)

2

21
22
23
24
25

68
69
70
71
72

43

22 (23.5/25.5/27.5/29.5)

2

RIGHT FRONT

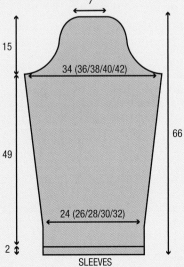

7

15

34 (36/38/40/42)

66

49

24 (26/28/30/32)

2

SLEEVES

73

19 Sweater

SIZES

34-36 (38-40, 42-44, 46-48, 50-52) (see Sizing Charts)

MATERIALS

Double knitting such as Laine & Coton from Phildar (50% wool and 50% cotton): **6 (6, 7, 7, 8)** balls of main colour (M), shown here in Sable shade; **4 (4, 4, 5, 5)** balls of contrast colour (A), shown in Persan • Pair each 3mm and 3.5mm needles

STITCHES USED

K1, P1 rib
Stocking stitch stripes: *4 rows using A, 4 rows using M*, rep from * to * (i.e. 8 rows in tot).

TENSION

It is essential to check your tension before starting your garment to ensure you get the right measurements.
On 3.5mm needles, 20 sts and 29 rows to 10cm in st st.

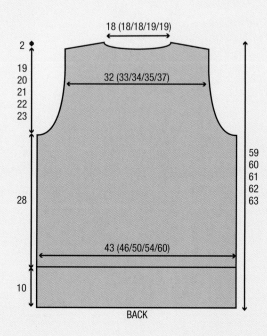

BACK

INSTRUCTIONS

BACK

With 3mm needles, cast on **88 (94, 102, 110, 122)** sts using M and work 10cm in K1, P1 rib then do 1 row P on WS using M.
Change to 3.5mm needles and cont in st st stripes (see Stitches Used).
When work measures 28cm from end of ribbing, shape armholes by casting off after 2 rows of A at beg of each row as follows:
34-36: 3 sts 4 times, 2 sts 4 times and 1 st twice
38-40: 4 sts twice, 3 sts twice, 2 sts 4 times and 1 st 4 times
42-44: 4 sts twice, 3 sts 4 times, 2 sts 4 times and 1 st 4 times
46-48: 5 sts twice, 4 sts twice, 3 sts 4 times, 2 sts twice and 1 st 4 times,
50-52: 5 sts twice, 4 sts twice, 3 sts 4 times, 2 sts 6 times and 1 st 4 times
66 (68, 70, 72, 76) sts remain.
When work measures **47 (48, 49, 50, 51)** cm from end of ribbing, shape shoulders by casting off at beg of every alt row at outside edge as follows: 3 sts once and 4 sts 3 times (4 sts 4 times; 5 sts once and 6 sts twice; 5 sts once and 6 sts twice; 6 sts twice and 7 sts once).
At the same time, shape neck by casting off the centre **14 (14, 14, 16, 16)** sts and cont, working one side at a time, casting off at neck edge every alt row: 6 sts once and 5 sts once.
Finish other side of neck to match.

FRONT

With 3mm needles, cast on **88 (94, 102, 110, 122)** sts using M and work 10cm in K1, P1 rib then do 1 row P on WS using M.
Change to 3.5mm needles and cont in st st stripes (see Stitches Used).
When work measures 28cm from end of ribbing, shape armholes by casting off (after 2 rows of A) at beg of each row as follows: 3 sts 4 times, 2 sts 4 times and 1 st twice (4 sts twice, 3 sts twice, 2 sts 4 times and 1 st 4 times, 4 sts twice, 3 sts 4 times, 2 sts 4 times and 1 st 4 times, 5 sts twice, 4 sts twice, 3 sts 4 times, 2 sts twice and 1 st 4 times, 5 sts twice, 4 sts twice, 3 sts 4 times, 2 sts 6 times and 1 st 4 times).
66 (68, 70, 72, 76) sts remain.
When work measures **37 (38, 39, 40, 41)** cm from end of ribbing, shape neck by casting off the centre **12 (12, 12, 14, 14)** sts then cont to work one side at a time and cast off at neck edge every alt row as follows: 4 sts once, 3 sts once, 2 sts once, 1 st twice and then 1 st on foll 4th row once.
When work measures **47 (48, 49, 50, 51)** cm from end of ribbing, shape shoulder by casting off at armhole edge every alt row as follows: 3 sts once and 4 sts 3 times (4 sts 4 times, 5 sts once and 6 sts twice, 5 sts once and 6 sts twice, 6 sts twice and 7 sts once).
Finish other side of neck.

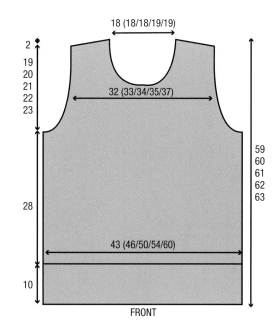

18 (18/18/19/19)

2

19
20
21
22
23

32 (33/34/35/37)

28

59
60
61
62
63

43 (46/50/54/60)

10

FRONT

SLEEVES

With 3mm needles, cast on **54 (58, 62, 66, 70)** sts using M and work 10cm in K1, P1 rib then do 1 row P on WS using M.

Change to 3.5mm needles, cont in st st stripes. Inc 1 in 3rd st from each end of row as follows: foll 16th row, once and every 14th row, 3 times (foll 16th row once and every 14th row 3 times; every 12th row 5 times; foll 12th row once and every 10th row 5 times; every 10th row 4 times and every 8th row 3 times).

62 (66, 72, 78, 84) sts.

When work measures 25cm in tot (74 rows), shape by casting off (after 2 rows using A) at beg of each row as follows: 2 sts twice, 1 st 40 times and 2 sts twice (2 sts 4 times, 1 st 36 times and 2 sts 4 times; 2 sts 8 times, 1 st 30 times and 2 sts 6 times; 2 sts 10 times, 1 st 24 times and 2 sts 10 times; 2 sts 14 times, 1 st 18 times and 2 sts 12 times).

When work measures 40cm from end of ribbing, loosely cast off rem 14 sts. Make left sleeve, reversing shaping.

NECKBAND

With 3mm needles, cast on **122 (122, 122, 124, 124)** sts using M and work 2cm in K1, P1 rib then work a P row on WS and a few rows of st st in another shade. Press these rows, they will be unpicked when attaching the neckband.

TO MAKE UP AND FINISH

Join shoulder, side and sleeve seams. Sew sleeves into armholes. Sew on neckband, st by st, using back st, on RS of work.

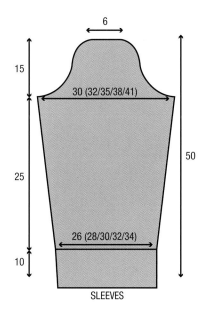

6

15

30 (32/35/38/41)

25

50

26 (28/30/32/34)

10

SLEEVES

20 Dress

In stocking stitch and intarsia
with crocheted trim.
Aran weight, such as Quiétude
and 5-ply or Sport weight yarn
such as Partner 3.5.

20 Dress

SIZES
34-36 (38-40, 42-44, 46-48, 50-52) (see Sizing Charts)

MATERIALS
Aran weight yarn such as Quiétude from Phildar (50% worsted wool and 50% acrylic): 8 (8, 9, 10, 10) balls of main colour (M), shown here in Camel shade; 1 (1, 1, 1, 1) ball of 1st contrast colour (A), shown in Écureuil; 1 (1, 1, 1, 1) ball of 2nd contrast colour (B), shown in Noir • 5-ply or Sport weight yarn such as Partner 3.5 from Phildar (50% polyamide, 25% acrylic and 25% polyamide): 1 (1, 1, 1, 2) balls in 3rd contrast colour (C), shown here in Curry • Pair each 3.5mm and 4mm needles • 3mm crochet hook • 1 button

STITCHES USED
K2, P2 rib
Stocking stitch
Intarsia patt worked in st st: see chart and legends

TENSION
It is essential to check your tension before starting your garment to ensure you get the right measurements.
On 4mm needles, 32 sts and 53 rows to 20cm in st st.
On 4mm needles, 35 sts and 53 rows to 20cm in intarsia patt.

INSTRUCTIONS
BACK
With 3.5mm needles, cast on **82 (86, 94, 98, 110)** sts using M. Work 2cm in K2, P2 rib, starting and ending first row and every odd row (RS) with K2. Change to 4mm needles and cont in st st, still using M. Inc **0 (0, 0, 2, 0)** sts evenly on first row.
82 (86, 94, 100, 110) sts.
When work measures 18cm from end of ribbing, dec 1 in 3rd st from each end of foll row, then rep: every 8th row 9 times (every 10th row 7 times; every 10th row 3 times and every 8th row 5 times; every 10th row 7 times; every 10th row 3 times and every 8th row 5 times).
62 (70, 76, 84, 92) sts remain.
When work measures 48cm from end of ribbing, inc 1 in 3rd st from each end of foll row, then rep: every 16th row twice (cont straight, cont straight, cont straight, cont straight).
68 (72, 78, 86, 94) sts.
When work measures 66cm from end of ribbing, shape armholes by casting off at beg of each row as follows: 3 sts twice, 2 sts 4 times and 1 st twice (3 sts twice, 2 sts 4 times and 1 st 4 times; 4 sts twice, 3 sts twice, 2 sts twice and 1 st 6 times; 4 sts twice, 3 sts 4 times, 2 sts twice and 1 st 6 times; 4 sts twice, 3 sts 4 times, 2 sts 6 times and 1 st 4 times).
52 (54, 54, 56, 58) sts remain.
When work measures **85 (86, 87, 88, 89)** cm from end of ribbing, shape shoulders by casting off at beg of every alt row at outside edge as follows: 2 sts twice and 3 sts twice (2 sts once and 3 sts 3 times; 2 sts once and 3 sts 3 times; 2 sts once and 3 sts 3 times; 4 sts 3 times).
At the same time, shape neck by casting off the centre **12 (12, 12, 14, 14)** sts and cont, working one side at a time, casting off 5 sts at neck edge every alt row, twice.
Finish other side of neck.

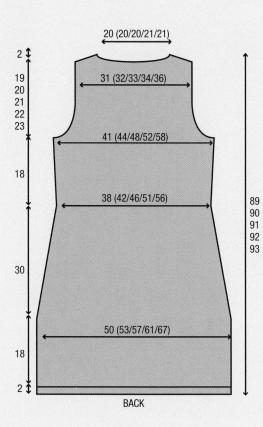

20 (20/20/21/21)

2

19
20
21
22
23

31 (32/33/34/36)

41 (44/48/52/58)

18

38 (42/46/51/56)

89
90
91
92
93

30

50 (53/57/61/67)

18

2

BACK

Dress cont'd

FRONT

With 3.5mm needles, cast on **82 (86, 94, 98, 110)** sts using M. Work 2cm in K2, P2 rib, starting and ending first row and every odd row (RS) with K2. Change to 4mm needles and cont in intarsia patt (see chart) worked in st st. Inc **6 (6, 6, 8, 6)** sts evenly on first row, positioning the 46 sts of patt in middle of work. **88 (92, 100, 106, 116)** sts.

When work measures 18cm from end of ribbing, dec 1 in 3rd st from each end of foll row, then rep: every 8th row, 9 times (every 10th row 7 times; every 10th row 3 times and every 8th row 5 times; every 10th row 7 times; every 10th row 3 times and every 8th row 5 times).

68 (76, 82, 90, 98) sts remain.

When work measures 48cm from end of ribbing, inc 1 in 3rd st from each end of foll row, then rep: every 16th row twice (cont straight; cont straight; cont straight; cont straight).

74 (78, 84, 92, 100) sts.

When work measures 66cm from end of ribbing, shape armholes by casting off the following number of sts at each armhole edge on alt rows: 3 sts once, 2 sts twice and 1 st once (3 sts once, 2 sts twice and 1 st twice; 4 sts once, 3 sts once, 2 sts once and 1 st 3 times; 4 sts once, 3 sts twice, 2 sts once and 1 st 3 times; 4 sts once, 3 sts twice, 2 sts 3 times and 1 st twice).

58 (60, 60, 62, 64) sts remain.

Meanwhile, when work measures **67 (68, 69, 70, 71)** cm from end of ribbing, split the work in 2 and cont, working one side at a time.

When work measures **75 (76, 77, 78, 79)** cm from end of ribbing, shape neck by casting off at centre opening edge every alt row as follows:

34-36, 38-40, 42-44: 3 sts twice, 2 sts twice, 1 st 7 times, then 1 st every 4th row, twice

46-48, 50-52: 3 sts twice, 2 sts 3 times, 1 st 6 times, then 1 st every 4th row, twice

When work measures **85 (86, 87, 88, 89)** cm from end of ribbing, shape shoulder by casting off at armhole edge every alt row as follows: 2 sts twice and 3 sts twice (2 sts once and 3 sts 3 times; 2 sts once and 3 sts 3 times; 2 sts once and 3 sts 3 times; 4 sts 3 times).

Finish other side of neck to match.

TO MAKE UP AND FINISH

Join shoulder and side seams. With 3mm crochet hook and M, do a row of crab st around armhole edges. With 3mm crochet hook, do a row of crab st around neck and front opening, matching colour changes. Work from left to right (if right-handed). Hold yarn at the back of the work. Insert the hook from front to back in the first stitch of the row. Draw up a loop and make one chain to begin. Moving to the right, insert hook into next stitch along from front to back. Yarn over. Draw up a loop. There are two loops on the hook. Yarn over and pull yarn through both loops as you would for a double crochet. Continue across the row inserting your hook to the right each time to make the next crab stitch. Make a button loop on front neckline and sew on a button.

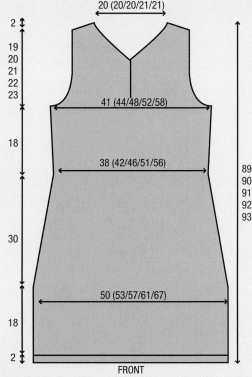

FRONT

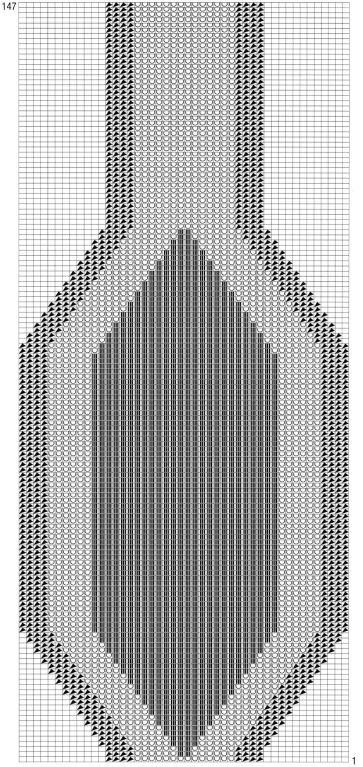

147

1

46 stitches

Repeat the 147 rows of chart

Main colour M
▶ 2nd contrast colour B
∪ 1st contrast colour A
‖ 3rd contrast colour C

The '70s

A new take on "Starsky and Hutch",
"Charlie's Angels", the classic hippy style,
a cool attitude and flares...

21 Fringe jacket

Stocking stitch and reverse stocking stitch.
Chunky yarns such as Terre Neuve and Neige.

22 Poncho

Crochet pattern.
3-ply such as Phil Light.

21 Fringe jacket

SIZES

S (15-17 yrs), M (42-44), L (46-48), XL (50-52), XXL (54-56) (see Sizing Charts)
S (M, L, XL, XXL)

MATERIALS

Chunky yarn such as Terre Neuve from Phildar (100% wool): **12 (13, 14, 15, 17)** balls of main colour (M), shown here in Renne shade • Chunky yarn such as Neige from Phildar (100% polyamide): **4 (4, 5, 5, 5)** balls of contrast colour (A), shown here in Lierre • Pair each 5.5mm, 6mm and 7mm needles • 1 x 60cm zip

STITCHES USED

Garter stitch (every row K)
Reverse stocking stitch (P on RS, K on WS)
Stocking stitch (K on RS, P on WS)

TENSION

It is essential to check your tension before starting your garment to ensure you get the right measurements.
On 7mm needles, 23 sts and 34 rows to 20cm in st st using Chunky yarn such as Terre Neuve (M).
On 6mm needles, 21 sts and 38 rows to 20cm in st st using Chunky yarn such as Neige (A).

INSTRUCTIONS

BACK

With 6mm needles, cast on **50 (53, 57, 61, 68)** sts using A and work 10cm in rev st st.
Change to 7mm needles and cont in st st, using M. Inc **6 (5, 7, 7, 6)** sts evenly on first row.
56 (58, 64, 68, 74) sts.
When work measures 35cm from end of rev st st, shape armholes by casting off at beg of each row as follows:
3 sts twice, 2 sts twice and 1 st 4 times (3 sts twice, 2 sts twice and 1 st 4 times; 3 sts twice, 2 sts 4 times and 1 st 6 times; 4 sts twice, 3 sts twice, 2 sts twice and 1 st 4 times; 4 sts twice, 3 sts 4 times, 2 sts twice and 1 st twice).
42 (44, 44, 46, 48) sts remain.
When work measures **43 (44, 45, 46, 47)** cm from end of rev st st, change to 6mm needles and do 2 rows in garter st using A (i.e. 1 ridge), then switch to 7mm needles and cont in st st using M.
When work measures **55 (56, 57, 58, 59)** cm from end of rev st st, shape shoulders by casting off at beg of every alt row at outside edge as follows: 4 sts twice and 3 sts once (4 sts 3 times; 4 sts 3 times; 4 sts 3 times; 4 sts twice and 5 sts once).
At the same time, shape neck by casting off centre **8 (8, 8, 10, 10)** sts then cont to work one side at a time, casting off 3 sts at neck edge every alt row, twice.
Finish other side of neck to match.

RIGHT FRONT

With 6mm needles, cast on **25 (27, 29, 31, 34)** sts using A and work 10cm in rev st st.
Change to 7mm needles and cont in st st, using M. Inc **3 (2, 3, 3, 3)** sts evenly on first row.
28 (29, 32, 34, 37) sts.
When work measures 35cm from end of rev st st, shape armhole by casting off at LH edge every alt row:
3 sts once, 2 sts once and 1 st twice (3 sts once, 2 sts once and 1 st twice; 3 sts once, 2 sts twice and 1 st 3 times; 4 sts once, 3 sts once, 2 sts once and 1 st twice; 4 sts once, 3 sts twice, 2 sts once and 1 st once).
21 (22, 22, 23, 24) sts remain.
When work measures **43 (44, 45, 46, 47)** cm from end of rev st st, change to 6mm needles and do 2 rows in garter st using A (i.e. 1 ridge), then switch to

7mm needles and cont in st st using M.

When work measures **49 (50, 51, 52, 53)** cm from end of rev st st, shape neck by casting off at RH edge every alt row:

3 sts once, 2 sts twice and 1 st twice, then 1 st on foll 4th row, once (3 sts once, 2 sts twice, 1 st twice, then 1 st on foll 4th row once; 3 sts once, 2 sts twice, 1 st twice then 1 st on foll 4th row once; 3 sts twice, 2 sts once, 1 st twice, 1 st on foll 4th row once; 3 sts twice, 2 sts once, 1 st twice, 1 st on foll 4th row once).

When work measures **55 (56, 57, 58, 59)** cm from end of rev st st, shape shoulder by casting off at armhole edge every alt row as follows: 4 sts twice and 3 sts once (4 sts 3 times; 4 sts 3 times; 4 sts 3 times; 4 sts twice and 5 sts once).

Make left front, reversing shaping.

SLEEVES

With 6mm needles, cast on **29 (31, 33, 35, 37)** sts using A and work 10cm in rev st st.

Change to 7mm needles and cont in st st, using M. Inc **3 (3, 3, 3, 5)** sts evenly on first row.

32 (34, 36, 38, 42) sts.

Inc 1 in the 3rd st from each end of row as follows: every 16th row, twice and on foll 14th row, once (every 12th row 4 times; every 12th row 4 times; every 10th row 5 times; every 10th row 5 times).

38 (42, 44, 48, 52) sts.

When work measures 35cm from end of rev st st, shape by casting off at beg of each row as follows: 2 sts twice, 1 st 22 times and 2 sts twice (2 sts 4 times, 1 st 18 times and 2 sts 4 times; 2 sts 6 times, 1 st 16 times and 2 sts 4 times; 2 sts 8 times, 1 st 12 times and 2 sts 6 times; 2 sts 10 times, 1 st 8 times and 2 sts 8 times).

When work measures 50cm from end of rev st st, loosely cast off rem 8 sts.

Knit second sleeve to match.

TO MAKE UP AND FINISH

Join shoulder, side and sleeve seams. Sew sleeves into armholes. With 5.5mm needles, pick up **56 (56, 56, 58, 58)** sts around neckline using A. Change to 6mm needles and work 14cm in st st then cast off loosely. Fold strands of M in half to make tassels that are about 18cm long and attach them by looping them under the 2 rows of garter st in A on back and front sections, spacing them one st apart.

Sew zip to front edges.

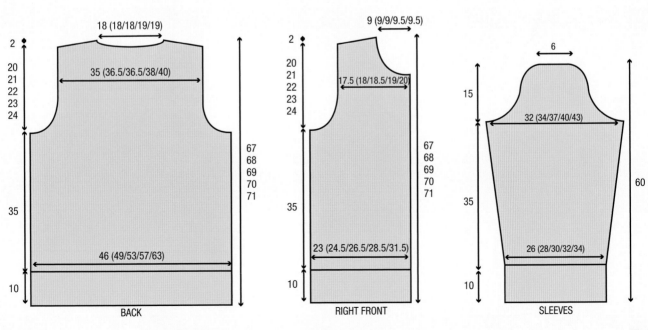

22 Poncho

ONE-SIZE

MATERIALS

A 3-ply yarn such as Phil Light from Phildar (53% acrylic, 29% polyamide and 18% wool): 6 balls, shown here in Bruyère shade • 5.5mm crochet hook

STITCHES USED

Chain st
Double crochet: Insert crochet hook into a st, draw through a loop, take yarn over hook (1yrh), draw yarn through both loops on hook.

Lattice stitch:
1st row: ch1 then dc rem sts.
2nd row: ch3 for 1tr,*2yrh, insert hook into foll st, draw through a loop, 1yrh, draw yarn through 2 loops, skip 1 st, 1yrh, insert hook into foll st, draw through 1 loop, °1yrh, draw yarn through 2 loops°, rep from ° to ° 4 times in tot; ch1, 1yrh, insert hook where 2 trs intersect, draw through a loop, 1 yrh, draw yarn through 2 loops, 1 yrh, draw yarn through last 2 loops,* rep from * to * and finish with 1tr.
3rd row: ch1 then dc rem sts.
Keep repeating rows 2 and 3.

Rib stitch:
1st row: dc entire row.
2nd row: dc entire row, inserting hook into back loop at top of st on previous row.
Keep repeating row 2.

Pattern stitch: *7 rows of lattice st, 13 rows of rib st*, rep from * to * (i.e. 20 rows in tot or 17cm).

TENSION

It is essential to check your tension before starting your garment to ensure you get the right measurements.
With 5.5mm hook, 5 lattices = 11cm
With 5.5mm hook, 7 rows of lattice st = 9.5cm
With 5.5mm hook, 28 sts and 35 rows to 20cm in rib st.

INSTRUCTIONS
BACK & FRONT

With 5.5mm crochet hook make a 75cm long foundation chain **(104 sts)** and continue to work in patt (see Stitches Used).
Fasten off when work measures 45cm.
Crochet second piece to match.

TO MAKE UP AND FINISH

Use coloured yarn as markers to indicate 15cm from right (see patt) then again for next 15cm.
Assemble back and front as follows: place A and B markers of 1st piece on A' and B' markers of 2nd piece and graft together.
Place A and B markers of 2nd piece on A' and B' markers of 1st piece and graft together.
Make 35cm-long tassels (length of finished tassels) from 2 strands folded in half, and attach them along the bottom edge.

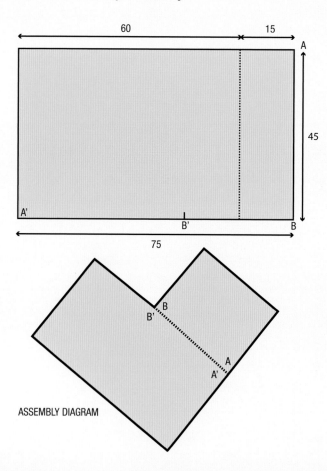

ASSEMBLY DIAGRAM

23 Sweater

Stocking stitch with ribbed edging.
Aran weight yarn such as
Beaugency and Chunky such as
Partner 6.

24 Hooded Sweater

Stocking stitch stripes
with French knitting trim.
Chunky yarn such as Partner 6.

23 Sweater

SIZES
34-36 (38-40, 42-44, 46-48, 50-52) (see Sizing Charts)

MATERIALS
Aran weight yarn such as Beaugency from Phildar (55% polyamide, 25% acrylic and 20% wool): **8 (9, 9, 10, 11)** balls of main colour (M), shown here in Persan shade • Chunky yarn such as Partner 6 from Phildar (50% polyamide, 25% worsted wool and 25% acrylic): **3 (3, 3, 4, 4)** balls of contrast colour (A), shown here in Canard • 5mm needles • 4mm crochet hook

STITCHES USED
K1, P1 rib
Stocking stitch
Double crochet

TENSION
It is essential to check your tension before starting your garment to ensure you get the right measurements.
On 5mm needles, 16 sts and 21 rows to 10cm in st st using Aran weight yarn such as Beaugency.

INSTRUCTIONS
BACK
With 5mm needles, cast on **70 (76, 82, 88, 98)** sts in Chunky yarn A and work 6cm in K1, P1 rib.
Still using 5mm needles, cont in st st using Aran weight yarn M.
When work measures 37cm from end of ribbing, shape armholes by casting off at beg of each row as follows: 3 sts twice, 2 sts 4 times and 1 st 4 times (4 sts twice, 3 sts twice, 2 sts twice and 1 st 4 times; 4 sts twice, 3 sts 4 times, 2 sts twice and 1 st twice; 4 sts twice, 3 sts 4 times, 2 sts 4 times and 1 st 4 times; 5 sts twice, 4 sts twice, 3 sts twice, 2 sts 4 times and 1 st 6 times).
52 (54, 56, 56, 60) sts remain.
When work measures **56 (57, 58, 59, 60)** cm from end of ribbing, shape shoulders by casting off at beg of every alt row at outside edge as follows: 4 sts 3 times (4 sts twice and 5 sts once; 4 sts once and 5 sts twice; 4 sts twice and 5 sts once; 5 sts 3 times).
At the same time, shape neck by casting off the centre **12 (12, 12, 14, 14)** sts and cont, working one side at a time, casting off 8 sts at neck edge on foll alt row.
Finish other side of neck to match.

FRONT
With 5mm needles, cast on **70 (76, 82, 88, 98)** sts using A and work 6cm in K1, P1 rib.
Still using 5mm needles, cont in st st using M.
When work measures 37cm from end of ribbing, shape armholes by casting off at beg of each row as follows: 3 sts twice, 2 sts 4 times and 1 st 4 times (4 sts twice, 3 sts twice, 2 sts twice and 1 st 4 times; 4 sts twice, 3 sts 4 times, 2 sts twice and 1 st twice; 4 sts twice, 3 sts 4 times, 2 sts 4 times and 1 st 4 times; 5 sts twice, 4 sts twice, 3 sts twice, 2 sts 4 times and 1 st 6 times).
52 (54, 56, 56, 60) sts remain.
When work measures **38 (39, 40, 41, 42)** cm from end of ribbing, split the work in 2 and cont, working one side at a time.
When work measures **49 (50, 51, 52, 53)** cm from end of ribbing, shape neck by casting off at front opening edge as follows:
34-36, 38-40, 42-44: 3 sts once then every alt row, 3 sts once, 2 sts twice, 1 st 3 times and then 1 st on foll 4th row once
46-48: 4 sts once then every alt row, 3 sts once, 2 sts twice, 1 st 3 times then 1 st on foll 4th row, once
50-52: 4 sts once then every alt row, 3 sts once, 2 sts twice, 1 st 3 times, then 1 st on foll 4th row once
When work measures **56 (57, 58, 59, 60)** cm from end of ribbing, shape shoulder by casting off at armhole edge every alt row as follows: 4 sts 3 times (4 sts twice and 5 sts once; 4 sts once and 5 sts twice; 4 sts twice and 5 sts once; 5 sts 3 times).
Finish other side of neck to match.

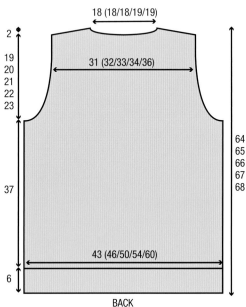

18 (18/18/19/19)

2
19
20
21
22
23

31 (32/33/34/36)

64
65
66
67
68

37

43 (46/50/54/60)

6

BACK

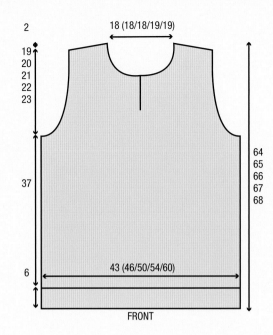

FRONT

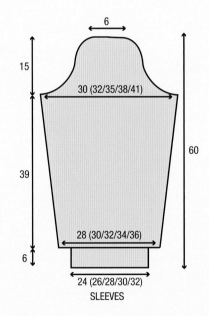

SLEEVES

SLEEVES

With 5mm needles, cast on **40 (44, 48, 50, 54)** sts using A and work 6cm in K1, P1 rib.

Still using 5mm needles, cont in st st, using M and inc 6 sts evenly on first row.

46 (50, 54, 56, 60) sts.

Inc 1 in the 3rd st from each end of row as follows: every 28th row twice (every 28th row twice; every 28th row twice; foll 22nd row once and every 20th row twice; foll 22nd row once and every 20th row 3 times).

50 (54, 58, 62, 68) sts.

When work measures 39cm from end of ribbing, shape by casting off at beg of each row as follows:

34-36: 2 sts 4 times, 1 st 10 times, work 2 rows straight then 1 st 12 times and 2 sts 4 times

38-40: 2 sts 6 times, 1 st 8 times, work 2 rows straight then 1 st 10 times and 2 sts 6 times

42-44: 3 sts twice, 2 sts 4 times, 1 st 8 times, work 2 rows straight then 1 st 10 times, 2 sts 4 times and 3 sts twice

46-48: 3 sts twice, 2 sts 6 times, 1 st 6 times, work 2 rows straight then 1 st 8 times, 2 sts 6 times and 3 sts twice

50-52: 3 sts 4 times, 2 sts 4 times, 1 st 16 times, 2 sts 4 times and 3 sts 4 times

When work measures 54cm from end of ribbing, loosely cast off rem 12 sts. Knit second sleeve to match.

COLLAR

With 5mm needles, cast on **86 (86, 86, 90, 90)** sts using A and work 14cm in K1, P1 rib. Work turning rows or short rows, leaving 7 sts unworked or on st holders at each end on alt rows, 4 times, then do one K row across all sts and a few rows of st st in another shade.

Press these rows, they will be unpicked when attaching the collar.

TO MAKE UP AND FINISH

Join shoulder, side and sleeve seams. Sew sleeves into armholes. With 4mm crochet hook, work 1 row dc around front opening. Sew collar around neckline, st by st, using back stitch on RS of work and positioning collar ends either side of front opening.

24 Hooded sweater

SIZES
34-36 (38-40, 42-44, 46-48, 50-52) (see Sizing Charts)

MATERIALS
Chunky yarn such as Partner 6 from Phildar (50% polyamide, 25% worsted wool and 25% acrylic) in 7 different shades: Phildar yarn shades shown here are given in brackets: **2 (3, 3, 3, 3)** balls of contrast colour A (Fuchsia); **3 (3, 4, 4, 4)** balls of contrast colour B (Bleuet); **3(4, 4, 4, 5)** balls of main colour M (Curry); **3 (3, 4, 4, 4)** balls of contrast colour C (Pavot); **3 (4, 4, 4, 5)** balls of contrast colour D (Orge); **2 (3, 3, 3, 3)** balls of contrast colour E (Billard); **2 (3, 3, 3, 3)** balls of contrast colour F (Noir) • Pair each 4.5mm and 5mm needles • 4.5mm double-pointed circular needle • French knitting bobbin

STITCHES USED
Stocking stitch stripes on front and back: *4 rows in E (Billard), 2 rows in D (Orge), 4 rows in C (Pavot), 4 rows in M (Curry), 4 rows in F (Noir), 2 rows in B (Bleuet), 2 rows in F (Noir), 2 rows in B (Bleuet), 2 rows in F (Noir), 2 rows in B (Bleuet), 4 rows in A (Fuchsia), 4 rows in E (Billard), 4 rows in D (Orge), 2 rows in C (Pavot), 2 rows in D (Orge), 2 rows in C (Pavot), 2 rows in D (Orge), 2 rows in C (Pavot), 4 rows in M (Curry), 4 rows in B (Bleuet), 4 rows in A (Fuchsia), 2 rows in D (Orge)*. 64 rows.
Rep from * to *

Stocking stitch stripes on sleeves: *4 rows in E (Billard), 4 rows in D (Orge), 4 rows in M (Curry), 4 rows in B (Bleuet), 4 rows in A (Fuchsia), 4 rows in C (Pavot), 4 rows in F (Noir)*. 28 rows.
Rep from * to *

Stocking stitch stripes on pouch pocket: *4 rows in M (Curry), 4 rows in B (Bleuet), 4 rows in A (Fuchsia), 4 rows in C (Pavot), 4 rows in F (Noir), 4 rows in E (Billard), 4 rows in D (Orge)*. 28 rows.
Rep from * to *

Stocking stitch stripes on hood: 8 rows in M (Curry), 4 rows in B (Bleuet), 8 rows in A (Fuchsia), 8 rows in C (Pavot), 4 rows in F (Noir), 8 rows in B (Bleuet), 4 rows in D (Orge), 8 rows in M (Curry), 8 rows in C (Pavot), 4 rows in E (Billard), 8 rows in D (Orge), 8 rows in M (Curry), 8 rows in B (Bleuet), 4 rows in A (Fuchsia) (i.e. 92 rows) then cont as follows:
4 rows in A (Fuchsia), 8 rows in B (Bleuet), 8 rows in M (Curry), 8 rows in D (Orge), 4 rows in E (Billard), 8 rows in C (Pavot), 8 rows in M (Curry), 4 rows in D (Orge), 8 rows in B (Bleuet), 4 rows in F (Noir), 8 rows in C (Pavot), 8 rows in A (Fuchsia), 4 rows in B (Bleuet), 8 rows in M (Curry).

TENSION
It is essential to check your tension before starting your garment to ensure you get the right measurements.
On 5mm needles, 16 sts and 26 rows to 10cm in st st stripes.

INSTRUCTIONS
BACK

With 4.5mm needles, cast on **70 (76, 82, 88, 98)** sts using M and work 2cm in st st then mark edge sts with a strand of different colour yarn to mark the rolled hem.

Change to 5mm needles and cont with st st stripes (see Stitches Used).

When work measures 46cm from rolled hem, mark edge sts with a strand of coloured yarn to mark armholes.

When work measures **65 (66, 67, 68, 69)** cm from rolled hem, shape shoulders by casting off at beg of every alt row at outside edge as follows: 4 sts once and 5 sts 3 times (5 sts twice and 6 sts twice; 6 sts 3 times and 7 sts once; 6 sts once and 7 sts 3 times; 8 sts 4 times).

At the same time, shape neck by casting off the centre **12 (12, 12, 14, 14)** sts and cont, working one side at a time, casting off 5 sts at neck edge every alt row, twice.

Finish other side of neck to match.

FRONT

With 4.5mm needles, cast on **70 (76, 82, 88, 98)** sts using M and work 2cm in st st then mark edge sts with a strand of different colour yarn to mark the rolled hem.

Change to 5mm needles and cont with st st stripes (see Stitches Used).

When work measures 46cm from rolled hem, mark edge sts with a strand of coloured yarn to mark armholes.

When work measures **48 (49, 50, 51, 52)** cm from rolled hem, split the work in 2 and cont, working one side at a time.

When work measures **58 (59, 60, 61, 62)** cm from rolled hem, shape neck by casting off at centre opening edge every alt row as follows:

34-36, 38-40, 42-44: 4 sts once, 3 sts once, 2 sts twice, 1 st 3 times and then 1 st every 4th row, twice

46-48, 50-52: 4 sts once, 3 sts once, 2 sts 3 times, 1 st twice and then 1 st every 4th row, twice

When work measures **65 (66, 67, 68, 69)** cm from end of rolled hem, shape shoulder by casting off at armhole edge every alt row as follows: 4 sts once and 5 sts 3 times (5 sts twice and 6 sts twice; 6 sts 3 times and 7 sts once; 6 sts once and 7 sts 3 times; 8 sts 4 times).

Finish other side of neck to match.

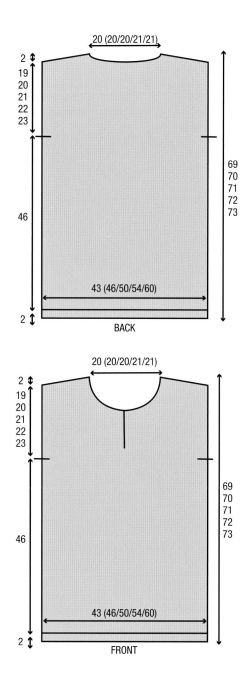

The '70s

Hooded sweater cont'd

SLEEVES

With 4.5mm needles, cast on **40 (44, 46, 50, 54)** sts using M and work 2cm in st st then mark edge sts with a strand of different colour yarn to mark the rolled hem.

Change to 5mm needles and cont in st st stripes (see Stitches Used). Inc 1 in the 3rd st from each end of row as follows: every 12th row, twice and every 10th row 9 times (every 12th row 6 times and every 10th row 4 times; every 10th row 11 times; every 12th row 4 times and every 10th row 6 times; foll 12th row once and every 10th row 9 times). **62 (64, 68, 70, 74)** sts.

When work measures **47.5 (47, 46, 45, 43)** cm from rolled hem, cast off loosely. Knit second sleeve to match.

HOOD

With 5mm needles, cast on **45 (45, 45, 47, 47)** sts, work in st st stripes (see Stitches Used) and inc at LH edge every alt row as follows: 1 st 3 times and 2 sts once. **50 (50, 50, 52, 52)** sts.

When work measures 32cm in tot, cast off at LH edge every alt row: 2 sts once and 1 st 3 times. **45 (45, 45, 47, 47)** sts remain.

When work measures 35cm in tot, inc at LH edge every alt row: 1 st 3 times and 2 sts once. **50 (50, 50, 52, 52)** sts.

When work measures 67cm in tot, cast off at LH edge every alt row: 2 sts once and 1 st 3 times.

When work measures 70cm in tot, cast off rem **45 (45, 45, 47, 47)** sts.

POUCH POCKET

With 5mm needles, cast on 50 sts using M and work in st st stripes (see Stitches Used).
Cont until work measures 16cm then cast off loosely.

POCKET EDGES

With 4.5mm needles cast on 26 sts using M and work 2cm in st st then do a few rows of st st in another shade.
Press these rows, they will be unpicked when attaching edges to pocket.
Knit second band to match.

TO MAKE UP AND FINISH

Join shoulder seams. Fit sleeves in armholes, between the coloured markers. Join side and sleeve seams. Join ends at crown of hood and sew hood round neckline. With 4.5mm double pointed circular needle and using M, pick up 148 sts around hood and along front opening. Work in st st and on foll alt row M1k each side of centre st (i.e. at front opening). When work measures 2cm in tot cast off loosely.

Sew pocket edges to sides of pocket (i.e. to 16cm sides) st by st, using back st on RS of work. Sew pocket onto front, 12cm from bottom. Using M, make 2 strips of French knitting, about 50cm long and sew them in place each side of the hood.

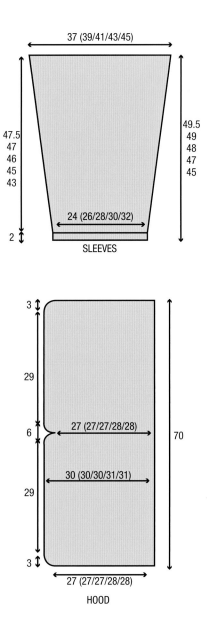

SLEEVES

HOOD

25 Collar Sweater

Stocking stitch, collar worked
in pattern stitch with rib and
crochet edging.
Sport weight such as Partner 3.5 and
3-ply such as Phil Light.

26 Skirt

Stocking stitch with rib
and crochet edging.
Sport weight such as
Partner 3.5

27 Tie-Neck Sweater

Tie-neck sweater in stocking stitch with ribbed edging. 3-ply such as Phil Light.

25 Collar sweater

SIZES
34-36 (38-40, 42-44, 46-48, 50-52) (see Sizing Charts)

MATERIALS
5-ply or Sport weight yarn such as Partner 3.5 from Phildar (50% polyamide, 25% worsted wool and 25% acrylic): **8 (9, 10, 10, 12)** balls in main colour (M), shown here in Mûre shade • A 3-ply yarn such as Phil Light from Phildar (53% acrylic, 29% polyamide and 18% wool): **1 (1, 1, 1, 1)** ball of contrast colour (A), shown here in Pensée • Pair each 3mm, 3.5mm and 5.5mm needles • 4mm crochet hook

STITCHES USED
K1, P1 rib
Stocking stitch
Pattern stitch: see chart and legends

TENSION
It is essential to check your tension before starting your garment to ensure you get the right measurements.
On 3.5mm needles, 24 sts and 30 rows to 10cm in st st
On 5.5mm needles, 16 sts and 23 rows to 10cm in pattern stitch

INSTRUCTIONS
BACK
With 3mm needles, cast on **106 (112, 122, 132, 146)** sts using M and work 5cm in K1, P1 rib.
Change to 3.5mm needles and cont in st st. Dec 1 in the 3rd st from each end of row, as follows: every 6th row, 5 times and every 4th row, 3 times (every 8th row, twice and every 6th row, 4 times; every 8th row, twice and every 6th row, 4 times; every 8th row, 5 times; every 8th row, twice and every 6th row, 4 times). **90 (100, 110, 122, 134)** sts remain.
Cont until work measures 15cm from end of ribbing then inc 1 in 3rd stitch from each end of foll row and then rep as follows: every 12th row, 4 times (foll 16th row once and every 14th row twice; foll 16th row once and every 14th row twice; foll 30th row once; foll 16th row once and every 14th row twice). **100 (108, 118, 126, 142)** sts.
When work measures 34cm from end of ribbing, shape armholes by casting off at beg of each row as follows:
34-36: 3 sts 4 times, 2 sts twice and 1 st 6 times
38-40: 4 sts twice, 3 sts 4 times, 2 sts twice and 1 st twice
42-44: 4 sts twice, 3 sts 4 times, 2 sts 4 times and 1 st 6 times
46-48: 5 sts twice, 4 sts twice, 3 sts 4 times, 2 sts 4 times and 1 st twice
50-52: 5 sts twice, 4 sts 4 times, 3 sts 4 times, 2 sts 4 times and 1 st 6 times
78 (82, 84, 86, 90) sts remain.
When work measures **52 (53, 54, 55, 56)** cm from end of ribbing, shape neck by casting off **26 (26, 26, 28, 28)** centre sts then cont to work one side at a time and cast off at neck edge every alt row as follows: 9 sts once, 5 sts once and 4 sts once.
When work measures **53 (54, 55, 56, 57)** cm from end of ribbing, shape shoulder by casting off at armhole edge every alt row as follows: 2 sts once and

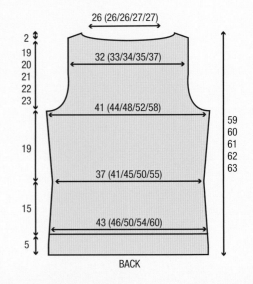

26 (26/26/27/27)

2
19
20
21
22
23

32 (33/34/35/37)

41 (44/48/52/58)

59
60
61
62
63

19

37 (41/45/50/55)

15

43 (46/50/54/60)

5

BACK

3 sts twice (3 sts twice and 4 sts once; 3 sts once and 4 sts twice; 3 sts once and 4 sts twice; 4 sts twice and 5 sts once).

Finish other side of neck.

FRONT

With 3mm needles, cast on **106 (112, 122, 132, 146)** sts using M and work 5cm in K1, P1 rib.

Change to 3.5mm needles and cont in st st. Dec 1 in the 3rd st from each end of row, as follows: every 6th row 5 times and every 4th row 3 times (every 8th row twice and every 6th row 4 times; every 8th row twice and every 6th row 4 times; every 8th row 5 times; every 8th row twice and every 6th row 4 times). **90 (100, 110, 122, 134)** sts remain.

When work measures 15cm from end of ribbing, inc 1 in 3rd stitch from each end of foll row and then rep as follows: every 12th row 4 times (foll 16th row once and every 14th row twice; foll 16th row once and every 14th row twice; foll 30th row once; foll 16th row once and every 14th row twice). **100 (108, 118, 126, 142)** sts.

When work measures 34cm from end of ribbing, shape armholes by casting off at beg of each row as follows:

34-36: 3 sts 4 times, 2 sts twice and 1 st 6 times

38-40: 4 sts twice, 3 sts 4 times, 2 sts twice and 1 st twice

42-44: 4 sts twice, 3 sts 4 times, 2 sts 4 times and 1 st 6 times

46-48: 5 sts twice, 4 sts twice, 3 sts 4 times 2 sts 4 times and 1 st twice

50-52: 5 sts twice, 4 sts 4 times, 3 sts 4 times, 2 sts 4 times and 1 st 6 times

78 (82, 84, 86, 90) sts remain.

When work measures 48 (49, 50, 51, 52) cm from end of ribbing, shape neck by casting off the **20 (20, 20, 22, 22)** centre sts then cont, working one side

at a time and cast off at neck edge every alt row as follows: 5 sts once, 4 sts twice, 3 sts once, 2 sts once and 1 st 3 times.

When work measures 53 (54, 55, 56, 57) cm from end of ribbing, shape shoulder by casting off at armhole edge every alt row as follows: 2 sts once and 3 sts twice (3 sts twice and 4 sts once; 3 sts once and 4 sts twice; 3 sts once and 4 sts twice; 4 sts twice and 5 sts once).

Finish other side of neck to match.

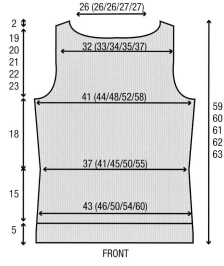

FRONT

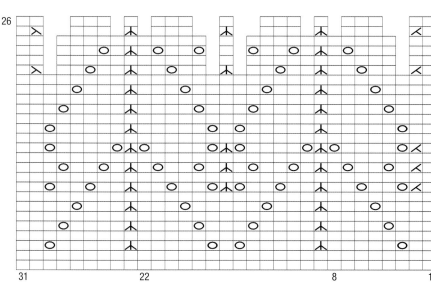

 K on RS; P on WS.

O YRN

⟋ K2tog

⟍ SL1,K1, PSSO.(Slip 1 knitwise, K1, pass slipped stitch over)

人 Vertical double decrease: Insert RHN through first 2 sts on LHN as if to knit them tog and slip both onto RHN at same time. Insert tip of LHN behind 2nd st to take first slipped st from RHN back onto LHN. Knit it tog with next st on LHN then pass 2nd slipped st over knitted st.

Collar sweater cont'd

SLEEVES

With 3mm needles, cast on **64 (70, 74, 78, 84)** sts using M and work 5cm in K1, P1 rib.

Change to 3.5mm needles and cont in st st. Inc 1 in the 3rd st from each end of row, as follows: every 20th row 5 times (every 24th row 4 times; every 18th row 4 times and every 16th row twice; every 14th row 6 times and every 12th row twice; every 14th row 6 times and every 12th row twice).

74 (78, 86, 94, 100) sts.

When work measures 40cm from end of ribbing, shape by casting off at beg of each row as follows:

34-36: 2 sts 8 times, 1 st 14 times, work 2 rows straight then 1 st 16 times and 2 sts 6 times

38-40: 2 sts 10 times, 1 st 12 times, work 2 rows straight then 1 st 14 times and 2 sts 8 times

42-44: 2 sts 14 times, 1 st 8 times, work 2 rows straight then 1 st 10 times and 2 sts 12 times

46-48: 3 sts 4 times, 2 sts 10 times, 1 st 6 times, work 2 rows straight then 1 st twice, work 2 rows straight then 1 st 6 times, 2 sts 10 times and 3 sts 4 times

50-52: 3 sts 6 times, 2 sts 8 times, 1 st 8 times, work 2 rows straight then 1 st 8 times, 2 sts 8 times and 3 sts 6 times

When work measures 55cm from end of ribbing, loosely cast off rem 16 sts. Knit second sleeve to match.

YOKE

With 5.5mm needles and 3-ply yarn A, cast on **171 (171, 171, 185, 185)** sts. Work in patt (see chart) as follows: patt from first st to 8th st of chart once; then patt from 9th st to 22nd st of chart **11 (11, 11, 12, 12)** times in total; then finish by working once from 23rd st to 31st st of chart. Once all 26 rows of chart have been completed, do 2 rows in st st then cast off loosely.

TO MAKE UP AND FINISH

Join shoulder, side and sleeve seams. Sew sleeves into armholes. Graft ends of yoke together then position it around neckline and attach it by working a row of dc using a 4mm crochet hook, inserting hook into both the yoke and sweater.

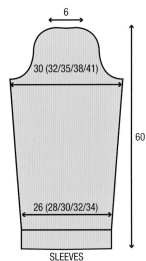

SLEEVES

26 Skirt

SIZES

34-36 (38-40, 42-44, 46-48, 50-52) (see Sizing Charts)

MATERIALS

5-ply or Sport weight yarn such as Partner 3.5 from Phildar (50% polyamide, 25% worsted wool and 25% acrylic): **6 (7, 7, 8, 8)** balls, shown here in Mûre shade • Pair each 2.5mm and 3.5mm needles • 2.5mm crochet hook • 1 x 15cm zip

STITCHES USED

K1, P1 rib
Stocking stitch
Double crochet: insert crochet hook into a st, draw through a loop, take yarn over hook (1yrh), draw yarn through both loops on hook.

TENSION

It is essential to check your tension before starting your garment to ensure you get the right measurements.
On 3.5mm needles, 23 sts and 30 rows to 10cm in st st.

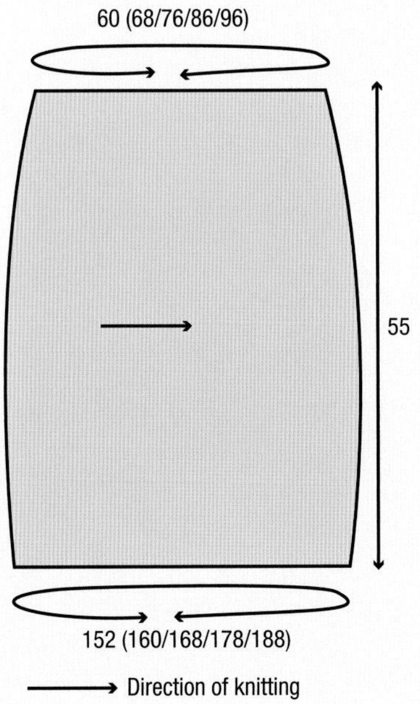

INSTRUCTIONS

The skirt is knitted in a single piece and crosswise, i.e. widthways (number of sts corresponds to skirt length).
With 3.5mm needles, cast on 120 sts and work in st st as follows:
*Work **14 (16, 18, 20, 24)** rows across all sts.
Work turning rows or short rows, leaving LH sts unworked or on holder every alt row: 6 sts 16 times and 3 sts once, therefore working 2 rows of: 114, 108, 102, 96, 90, 84, 78, 72, 66, 60, 54, 48, 42, 36, 30, 24 and 21 sts.
Take back 6 LH sts every alt row 6 times, therefore working 2 rows of 27, 33, 39, 45, 51 and 57 sts.
Work **30 (34, 38, 44, 48)** rows across all sts.
Work turning rows or short rows, leaving LH sts unworked or on holder every alt row: 6 sts 16 times and 3 sts once, therefore working 2 rows of: 114, 108, 102, 96, 90, 84, 78, 72, 66, 60, 54, 48, 42, 36, 30, 24 and 21 sts.
Take back 6 LH sts every alt row: 6 times, therefore working 2 rows of 27, 33, 39, 45, 51 and 57 sts.
Work **16 (18, 20, 22, 24)** rows across all sts.*
Rep from * to *, i.e.**152 (160, 168, 178, 188)** rows, twice more, making 3 repeats in total.
When work measures **152 (160, 168, 178, 188)** cm (measured on RH side), cast off loosely.
Work measures **60 (68, 76, 86, 96)** cm in tot (measured on LH side).

WAISTBAND

On 2.5mm needles, 13 sts and 32 rows to 10cm in K1, P1 rib.
With 2.5mm needles, cast on 13 sts and work **60 (68, 76, 86, 96)** cm in K1, P1 rib then cast off.

TO MAKE UP AND FINISH

Join skirt, leaving a 10cm opening for zip.
Graft waistband to top edge of skirt.
With a 2.5mm crochet hook, do 1 row of dc along opening.
Sew in zip.

60 (68/76/86/96)

55

152 (160/168/178/188)

Direction of knitting

27 Tie-neck sweater

SIZES
34-36 (38-40, 42-44, 46-48, 50-52) (see Sizing Charts)

MATERIALS
A 3-ply yarn such as Phil Light from Phildar (53% acrylic 29% polyamide and 18% wool): **6 (6, 7, 7, 8)** balls, shown here in Bengale shade • Pair each 4.5mm and 5mm needles

STITCHES USED
K1, P1 rib
Stocking stitch

TENSION
It is essential to check your tension before starting your garment to ensure you get the right measurements.
On 5mm needles, 32 sts and 55 rows to 20cm in st st using a double strand of yarn.

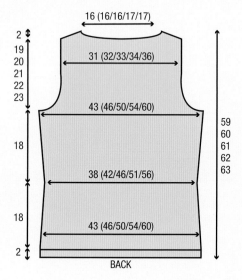

2
19
20
21
22
23

16 (16/16/17/17)

31 (32/33/34/36)

43 (46/50/54/60)

18

38 (42/46/51/56)

18

43 (46/50/54/60)

2

59
60
61
62
63

BACK

INSTRUCTIONS
BACK
With 4.5mm needles, cast on **70 (76, 82, 88, 98)** sts using a double strand of yarn and work 2cm in K1, P1 rib.
Change to 5mm needles and cont in st st using a double strand of yarn. Dec 1 in the 3rd st from each end of row, as follows: every 10th row 4 times (foll 14th row once then every 12th row twice; foll 14th row once then every 12th row twice; foll 18th row once and foll 16th row once; foll 14th row once then every 12th row twice).
62 (70, 76, 84, 92) sts remain.
When work measures 18cm from end of ribbing, inc 1 in 3rd st from each end of next row then rep as follows: foll 14th row once and every 12th row twice (every 16th row twice; every 16th row twice; foll 24th row once; every 16th row twice).
70 (76, 82, 88, 98) sts remain.
When work measures 36cm from end of ribbing, shape armholes by casting off at beg of each row as follows:
34-36: 3 sts twice, 2 sts 4 times and 1 st 4 times
38-40: 4 sts twice, 3 sts twice, 2 sts twice and 1 st 4 times
42-44: 4 sts twice, 3 sts 4 times, 2 sts twice and 1 st 4 times,
46-48: 4 sts twice, 3 sts 4 times, 2 sts 4 times and 1 st 4 times,
50-52: 5 sts twice, 4 sts twice, 3 sts 4 times, 2 sts twice and 1 st 4 times).
52 (54, 54, 56, 60) sts remain.
When work measures **55 (56, 57, 58, 59)** cm from end of ribbing, shape shoulders by casting off at beg of every alt row at outside edge as follows:
3 sts 3 times and 4 sts once (3 sts twice and 4 sts twice; 3 sts twice and 4 sts twice; 3 sts twice and 4 sts twice; 4 sts 4 times).
At the same time, shape neck by casting off the centre **10 (10, 10, 12, 12)** sts and cont, working one side at a time, casting off 4 sts at neck edge every alt row, twice.
Finish other side of neck to match.

FRONT
With 4.5mm needles, cast on **70 (76, 82, 88, 98)** sts using a double strand of yarn and work 2cm in K1, P1 rib.
Change to 5mm needles and cont in st st using a double strand of yarn. Dec 1 in the 3rd st from each end of row, as follows: every 10th row 4 times (foll 14th row once then every 12th row twice; foll 14th row once then every 12th row twice; foll 18th row once and foll 16th row once; foll 14th row once then every 12th row twice).
62 (70, 76, 84, 92) sts remain.
When work measures 18cm from end of ribbing, inc 1 in 3rd st from each end of next row then rep as follows: foll 14th row once and every 12th row twice (every 16th row twice; every 16th row twice; foll 24th row once; every 16th row twice).
70 (76, 82, 88, 98) sts.

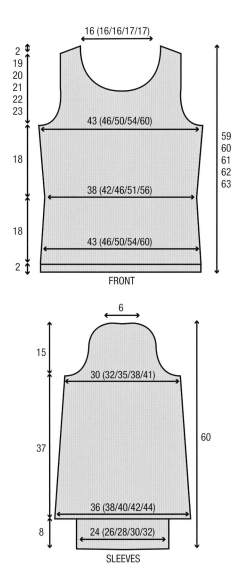

FRONT

SLEEVES

When work measures 36cm from end of ribbing, shape armholes by casting off at beg of each row as follows:

34-36: 3 sts twice, 2 sts 4 times and 1 st 4 times

38-40: 4 sts twice, 3 sts twice, 2 sts twice and 1 st 4 times

42-44: 4 sts twice, 3 sts 4 times, 2 sts twice and 1 st 4 times

46-48: 4 sts twice, 3 sts 4 times, 2 sts 4 times and 1 st 4 times

50-52: 5 sts twice, 4 sts twice, 3 sts 4 times, 2 sts twice and 1 st 4 times

52 (54, 54, 56, 60) sts remain.

When work measures **41 (42, 43, 44, 45)** cm from end of ribbing, shape neck by casting off centre **6 (6, 6, 8, 8)** sts then cont, working on one side at a time and cast off at neck edge every alt row as follows: 2 sts once, 1 st twice, 1 st every 4th row, twice, 1 st on foll 6th row once then 1 st every 8th row, 3 times.

When work measures **55 (56, 57, 58, 59)** cm from end of ribbing, shape shoulder by casting off at armhole edge every alt row as follows: 3 sts 3 times and 4 sts once (3 sts twice and 4 sts twice; 3 sts twice and 4 sts twice; 3 sts twice and 4 sts twice; 4 sts 4 times).

Finish other side of neck to match.

SLEEVES

With 4.5mm needles, cast on **40 (44, 46, 50, 54)** sts using a double strand of yarn and work 8cm in K1, P1 rib.

Change to 5mm needles, cont in st st and inc **20 (18, 20, 20, 18)** sts evenly on first row.

60 (62, 66, 70, 72) sts remain.

Dec 1 in the 3rd st from each end of row as follows: every 18th row 3 times and every 16th row twice (foll 22nd row once then every 20th row 3 times; foll 22nd row once then every 20th row 3 times; foll 22nd row once then every 20th row 3 times; every 34th row twice).

50 (54, 58, 62, 68) sts remain.

When work measures 37cm from end of ribbing, shape by casting off at beg of each row as follows:

34-36: 2 sts twice, 1 st 12 times, *work 2 rows straight then 1 st twice*, rep from * to * 4 times in tot, 1 st 10 times and 2 sts twice

38-40: 2 sts twice, 1 st 16 times, work 2 rows straight then 1 st twice, work 2 rows straight then 1 st 16 times and 2 sts twice

42-44: 2 sts 4 times, 1 st 14 times, work 2 rows straight then 1 st twice, work 2 rows straight then 1 st 14 times and 2 sts 4 times

46-48: 2 sts 6 times, 1 st 14 times, work 2 rows straight then 1 st 16 times and 2 sts 4 times

50-52: 3 sts twice, 2 sts 4 times, 1 st 14 times, work 2 rows straight then 1 st 14 times, 2 sts 4 times and 3 sts twice

When work measures 52cm from end of ribbing, loosely cast off rem 12 sts. Knit second sleeve to match.

TIE-NECK

With 5mm needles cast on 17 sts using a single strand of yarn and work 144cm in K1, P1 rib then cast off loosely in rib.

TO MAKE UP AND FINISH

Join shoulder, side and sleeve seams. Sew sleeves into armholes. Mark the middle of the tie-neck collar and position it centrally at the back then sew it in place around neckline, leaving ends free for tying in a bow.

28 Cowl Neck Sweater

Intarsia with ribbed edges.
3-ply such as Phil Light.

28 Cowl neck sweater

SIZES

34-36 (38-40, 42-44, 46-48, 50-52) (see Sizing Charts)

MATERIALS

A 3-ply yarn such as Phil Light from Phildar (53% acrylic, 29% polyamide and 18% wool): **3 (4, 4, 4, 5)** balls of main colour (M), shown here in Poivre; **2 (2, 2, 2, 2)** balls of 1st contrast colour (A) shown in Chantilly; **2 (2, 2, 2, 3)** balls of 2nd contrast colour (B) shown in Givre; **3 (3, 3, 3, 3)** balls of 3rd contrast colour (C) shown in Pêche • Pair of 4mm needles

STITCHES USED

K1, P1 rib

Intarsia colourwork in stocking stitch,

Stocking stitch stripes on right sleeve: 42 (42, 42, 40, 38) rows using a double strand of B (Givre), **44 (44, 42, 42, 40)** rows using a double strand of M (Poivre) and **44 (44, 42, 42, 40)** rows using a double strand of C (Pêche).

Stocking stitch stripes on left sleeve: 42 (42, 42, 40, 38) rows using a double strand of B (Givre), **44 (44, 42, 42, 40)** rows using a double strand of A (Chantilly) and **44 (44, 42, 42, 40)** rows using a double strand of M (Poivre).

TENSION

It is essential to check your tension before starting your garment to ensure you get the right measurements.

On 4mm needles, 18 sts and 30 rows to 10cm in intarsia, worked in st st using a double strand of yarn.

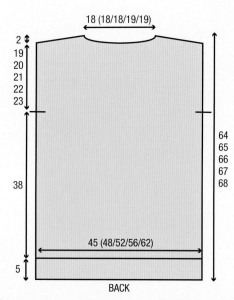

18 (18/18/19/19)

2
19
20
21
22
23

64
65
66
67
68

38

45 (48/52/56/62)

5

BACK

INSTRUCTIONS

BACK

With 4mm needles, cast on **84 (88, 96, 102, 114)** sts using a double strand of M. Work 5cm in K1, P1 rib.

Still using 4mm needles, cont in intarsia, work in st st, and dec **0 (1, 0, 0, 0)** st on first row, setting patt as follows:

28 (29, 32, 34, 38) sts using a double strand of C, **28 (29, 32, 34, 38)** sts using a double strand of M and **28 (29, 32, 34, 38)** sts using a double strand of A. **84 (87, 96, 102, 114)** sts.

When work measures 20cm from end of ribbing, cont in following patt: **28 (29, 32, 34, 38)** sts using a double strand of M, **28 (29, 32, 34, 38)** sts using a double strand of B and **28 (29, 32, 34, 38)** sts using a double strand of C.

When work measures 38cm from end of ribbing, mark edge sts with a strand of coloured yarn to mark armholes.

When work measures 40cm from end of ribbing, cont in following patt: **28 (29, 32, 34, 38)** sts using a double strand of C, **28 (29, 32, 34, 38)** sts using a double strand of A and **28 (29, 32, 34, 38)** sts using a double strand of B.

When work measures **57 (58, 59, 60, 61)** cm from end of ribbing, shape shoulders by casting off at beg of every alt row at outside edge as follows: 6 sts twice and 7 sts twice (7 sts 4 times; 8 sts 4 times; 8 sts twice and 9 sts twice; 10 sts 4 times).

At the same time, shape neck by casting off the centre **10 (9, 10, 12, 12)** sts and cont, working one side at a time, casting off at neck edge every alt row: 6 sts once and 5 sts once.

Finish other side of neck to match.

FRONT

With 4mm needles, cast on **84 (88, 96, 102, 114)** sts using a double strand of M. Work 5cm in K1, P1 rib.

Still using 4mm needles, cont in intarsia and dec **0 (1, 0, 0, 0)** st on first row, setting patt as follows:

28 (29, 32, 34, 38) sts using a double strand of C, **28 (29, 32, 34, 38)** sts using a double strand of M and **28 (29, 32, 34, 38)** sts using a double strand of A. **84 (87, 96, 102, 114)** sts.

When work measures 20cm from end of ribbing, cont in following patt: **28 (29, 32, 34, 38)** sts using a double strand of M, **28 (29, 32, 34, 38)** sts using a double strand of B and **28 (29, 32, 34, 38)** sts using a double strand of C.

When work measures 38cm from end of ribbing, mark edge sts with a strand of coloured yarn to mark armholes.

When work measures 40cm from end of ribbing, cont in following patt: **28 (29, 32, 34, 38)** sts using a double strand of C, **28 (29, 32, 34, 38)** sts using a double strand of A and **28 (29, 32, 34, 38)** sts using a double strand of B.

When work measures **50 (51, 52, 53, 54)** cm from end of ribbing, shape neck by casting off centre **8 (7, 8, 10, 10)** sts then cont, working one side at a time and cast off at neck edge every alt row as follows:

3 sts once, 2 sts twice then 1 st every 4th row, 4 times.

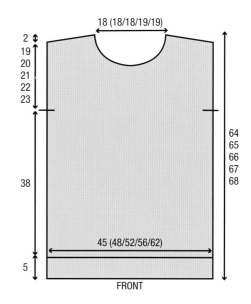

FRONT

18 (18/18/19/19)

2
19
20
21
22
23

38

5

64
65
66
67
68

45 (48/52/56/62)

When work measures **57 (58, 59, 60, 61)** cm from end of ribbing, shape shoulders by casting off at beg of every alt row at outside edge as follows: 6 sts twice and 7 sts twice (7 sts 4 times, 8 sts 4 times, 8 sts twice and 9 sts twice, 10 sts 4 times).

Finish other side of neck to match.

RIGHT SLEEVE

With 4mm needles, cast on **46 (48, 52, 56, 60)** sts using a double strand of M and work 5cm in K1, P1 rib.

Still using 4mm needles, cont in st st stripes (see Stitches Used). Inc 1 in the 3rd st from each end of row, as follows: every 12th row 5 times and every 10th row 6 times (every 10th row 12 times; every 10th row 11 times and on foll 8th row once; every 10th row 10 times and every 8th row twice; every 10th row 7 times and every 8th row 5 times).

When work measures **43.5 (43, 42, 41, 39)** cm from end of ribbing, loosely cast off the **68 (72, 76, 80, 84)** sts.

Knit left sleeve with corresponding stripe patt (see Stitches Used).

COLLAR

With 4mm needles, cast on **102 (102, 102, 106, 106)** sts using a double strand of M and work 25cm in K1, P1 rib then work a K row on RS and a few rows of st st in another shade.

Press these rows, they will be unpicked when attaching the collar.

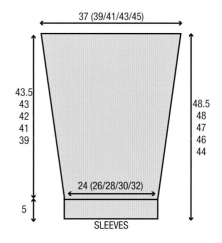

SLEEVES

37 (39/41/43/45)

43.5
43
42
41
39

48.5
48
47
46
44

5

24 (26/28/30/32)

TO MAKE UP AND FINISH

Join shoulder seams. Fit sleeves in armholes, between coloured markers. Join side and sleeve seams. Join ends of collar, leaving with half the seam on one side of the work and half on the other side so it is hidden when collar is turned down. Sew collar to neckline, st by st, using back stitch, on RS of work.

29 Jacket

Stocking stitch and Fair Isle with K1,
P1 and K2, P2 rib.
Chunky yarn such as Rapido.

29 Jacket

SIZES

S (15-17 yrs), M (42-44), L (46-48), XL (50-52), XXL (54-56) (see Sizing Charts)
S (M, L, XL, XXL)

MATERIALS

Chunky yarn such as Rapido from Phildar (50% polyamide, 25% worsted wool
and 25% acrylic): **18 (19, 21, 23, 25)** balls of main colour (M), shown here in
Chanvre shade; **1 (2, 2, 2, 2)** balls of 1st contrast colour (A), shown in Caramel;
2 (2, 3, 3, 3) balls of 2nd contrast colour (B), shown in Noir • Pair each 7mm
and 8mm needles • 6 Buttons

STITCHES USED

K1, P1 rib
K2, P2 rib
Stocking stitch
Fair Isle patt worked in st st: see chart and legends

TENSION

It is essential to check your tension before starting your garment to ensure
you get the right measurements.
On 8mm needles, 21 sts and 33 rows to 20cm in st st
On 8mm needles, 23 sts and 29 rows to 20cm in Fair Isle patt.

INSTRUCTIONS

BACK

With 7mm needles, cast on **50 (54, 58, 62, 66)** sts using M. Work 6cm in K2,
P2 rib, starting and ending first row and every odd row (RS) with K2.
Change to 8mm needles and cont in Fair Isle patt as shown in chart 1. Inc **6 (6,
6, 6, 8)** sts evenly on first row.
56 (60, 64, 68, 74) sts.
Once the 6 rows in chart 1 are completed, cont in st st using M and dec **4 (6,
6, 6, 8)** sts evenly on first row.
52 (54, 58, 62, 66) sts remain.
When work measures 37cm from end of ribbing, work in Fair Isle, following patt
in chart 2 and inc **4 (6, 6, 6, 8)** sts evenly on first row.
56 (60, 64, 68, 74) sts.
Once the 5 rows of chart 2 are completed, foll chart 3 then chart 4.
Meanwhile, when work measures 45cm from end of ribbing, shape armholes
by casting off at beg of each row as follows: 2 sts twice and 1 st 6 times (3 sts
twice, 2 sts twice and 1 st twice; 3 sts twice, 2 sts twice and 1 st twice; 3 sts
twice, 2 sts twice and 1 st 4 times; 3 sts twice, 2 sts 4 times and 1 st twice).
46 (48, 52, 54, 58) sts remain.
Once the 5 rows in chart 4 are completed, cont in st st using M and dec **4 (4,
6, 4, 6)** sts evenly on first row.
42 (44, 46, 50, 52) sts remain.
When work measures **66 (67, 68, 69, 70)** cm from end of ribbing, shape
shoulders by casting off at outside edge at beg of each alt row as follows: 4 sts
3 times (4 sts 3 times; 4 sts twice and 5 sts once; 4 sts once and 5 sts twice;
5 sts 3 times).
At the same time, shape neck by casting off the centre **6 (8, 8, 10, 10)** sts
and cont, working one side at a time, casting off 3 sts at neck edge every alt
row, twice.
Finish other side of neck to match.

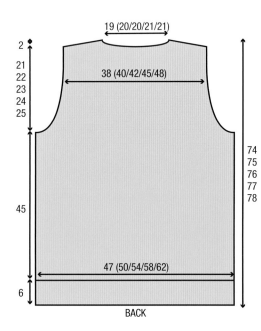

BACK

RIGHT FRONT

With 7mm needles, cast on **23 (27, 27, 31, 31)** sts using M. Work 6cm in K2, P2 rib, starting first row and every odd row (RS) with K3 and ending with K2. Change to 8mm needles and cont in Fair Isle patt as shown in chart 1. Inc **2 (0, 2, 0, 3)** sts evenly on first row.

25 (27, 29, 31, 34) sts.

Once the 6 rows in chart 1 are completed, cont in st st using M and dec **2 (3, 3, 3, 4)** sts evenly on first row.

23 (24, 26, 28, 30) sts remain.

When work measures 37cm from end of ribbing, work in Fair Isle, following patt in chart 2 and inc **2 (3, 3, 3, 4)** sts evenly on first row.

25 (27, 29, 31, 34) sts.

Once the 5 rows of chart 2 are completed, foll chart 3 then chart 4.

Meanwhile, when work measures **43 (44, 45, 46, 47)** cm from end of ribbing, shape front slope by casting off 1 st at RH edge and rep as follows: every alt row once, then every 4th row 6 times (every alt row 3 times then every 4th row 5 times; every alt row 5 times then every 4th row 4 times; every alt row 5 times then every 4th row 4 times; every alt row 7 times then every 4th row 3 times).

Meanwhile when work measures 45cm from end of ribbing, shape armhole by casting off at LH edge every alt row: 2 sts once and 1 st 3 times (3 sts once, 2 sts once and 1 st once; 3 sts once, 2 sts once and 1 st once; 3 sts once, 2 sts once and 1 st twice; 3 sts once, 2 sts twice and 1 st once).

Once the 5 rows in chart 4 are completed, cont in st st using M.

When work measures **66 (67, 68, 69, 70)** cm from end of ribbing, shape shoulder by casting off at armhole edge every alt row as follows: 4 sts 3 times (4 sts 3 times; 4 sts twice and 5 sts once; 4 sts once and 5 sts twice; 5 sts 3 times).

Make left front, reversing shaping.

SLEEVES

With 7mm needles, cast on **30 (30, 34, 34, 38)** sts using M. Work 6cm in K2, P2 rib, starting and ending first row and every odd row (RS) with K2. Change to 8mm needles and cont in Fair Isle patt as shown in chart 1. Inc **2 (4, 2, 4, 4)** sts evenly on first row.

32 (34, 36, 38, 42) sts.

Inc 1 each end of row as follows: every 10th row 6 times (every 10th row 6 times; every 10th row 6 times; every 10th row 6 times; every 12th row 5 times). **44 (46, 48, 50, 52)** sts.

Meanwhile, when work measures 36cm from end of ribbing, work in Fair Isle, following patt on chart 2, followed by chart 3 then 4.

Once the 5 rows in chart 4 are completed, cont in st st using M.

When work measures 44cm from end of ribbing, shape by casting off at beg of each row as follows:

34-36: 2 sts 6 times, 1 st 14 times and 2 sts 4 times

38-40: 2 sts 6 times, 1 st 12 times and 2 sts 6 times,

42-44: 2 sts 8 times, 1 st 10 times and 2 sts 6 times

46-48: 2 sts 8 times, 1 st 8 times and 2 sts 8 times

50-52: 3 sts twice, 2 sts 6 times, 1 st 8 times and 2 sts 8 times

Cont until work measures 60cm from end of ribbing then loosely cast off rem 10 sts.

Knit second sleeve to match.

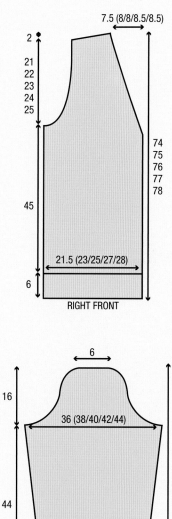

RIGHT FRONT

7.5 (8/8/8.5/8.5)

2
21
22
23
24
25
74
75
76
77
78
45
21.5 (23/25/27/28)
6

SLEEVES

6
16
36 (38/40/42/44)
44
66
26 (28/30/32/34)
6

The '70s

Jacket cont'd

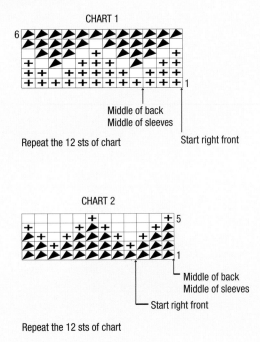

CHART 1

6

Middle of back
Middle of sleeves

Repeat the 12 sts of chart   Start right front

CHART 2

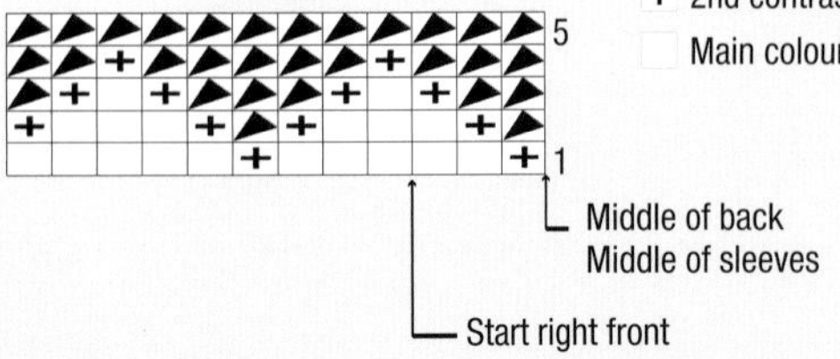

5

1

Middle of back
Middle of sleeves

Start right front

Repeat the 12 sts of chart

CHART 3

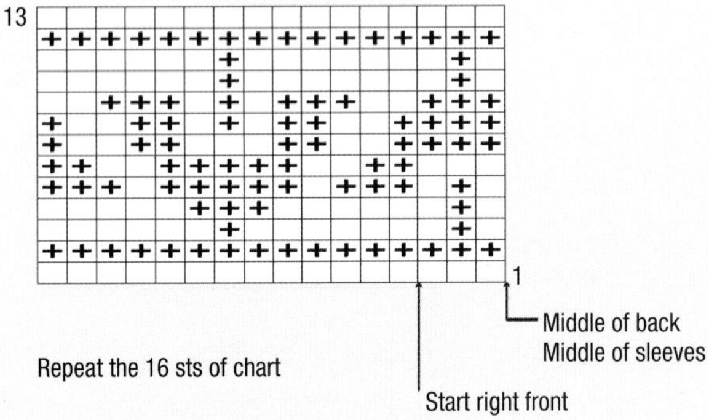

13

1

Middle of back
Middle of sleeves

Start right front

Repeat the 16 sts of chart

CHART 4

5

1

▶ 1st contrast colour (A)
+ 2nd contrast colour (B)
☐ Main colour (M)

Middle of back
Middle of sleeves

Start right front

Repeat the 12 sts of chart

COLLAR

With 7mm needles, cast on **119 (123, 125, 127, 129)** sts using M and work in K2, P2 rib, starting first row and every odd row (RS) with K3 and ending with K2 (K2, P2, K2, P2).

When work measures 4cm, work short rows as follows: leave **64 (65, 66, 68, 70)** RH sts (i.e. K3 end) unworked on holder, then leave more sts on holder every alt row: 4 sts 10 times and 5 sts once.

Work one row across all sts then a few rows of st st in another shade. Press these rows, they will be unpicked when attaching the collar.

Knit a second piece, reversing shaping and make 6 buttonholes over 2 sts on the 3rd row, positioning first buttonhole 3 sts from edge and the rest spaced **10 (10, 10, 11, 11)** sts apart.

Finish as before.

BELT

With 7mm needles cast on 7 sts using M and work **190 (190, 195, 195, 195)** cm in K1, P1 rib then cast off loosely in rib.

BELT LOOPS

With 7mm needles cast on 5 sts using M and work 5cm in K1, P1 rib then cast off loosely in rib.

Make a second loop in same way.

TO MAKE UP AND FINISH

Join shoulder, side and sleeve seams. Sew sleeves into armholes. Sew belt loops on at side seams, 30cm up from bottom.

Graft ends of collar together (i.e. K2 or P2 ends), then sew it along neckline and front edges, st by st using back stitch on RS of work. Sew on buttons.

30 Polo-Neck Sweater

Stocking stitch and Fair
Isle with K2, P2 ribbing.
Chunky yarn such as
Partner 6.

30 Polo-neck sweater

SIZES
34-36 (38-40, 42-44, 46-48, 50-52) (see Sizing Charts)

MATERIALS
Chunky yarn such as Partner 6 from Phildar (50% polyamide, 25% worsted wool and 25% acrylic): **10 (10, 11, 13, 14)** balls of main colour (M), shown here in Écru shade; **2 (2, 2, 2, 2)** balls of 1st contrast colour (A), shown in Noir; **3 (3, 3, 4, 4)** balls of 2nd contrast colour (B), shown in Châtaigne • Pair each 5.5mm and 6mm needles • 6mm double pointed circular needle

STITCHES USED
K2, P2 rib
Stocking stitch
Fair Isle patt worked in st st: see chart and legends

TENSION
It is essential to check your tension before starting your garment to ensure you get the right measurements.
On 6mm needles, 15 sts and 23 rows to 10cm in st st
On 6mm needles, 15 sts to 10cm in Fair Isle patt
On 6mm needles, the 29 rows of yoke collar = 15.5cm

CHART 1

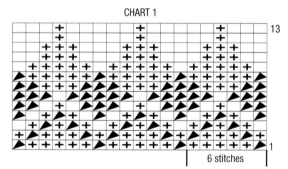

13

1

6 stitches

Repeat the 6 sts of chart

▶ 1st contrast colour (A)
+ 2nd contrast colour (B)
  Main colour (M)

INSTRUCTIONS
BACK
With 5.5mm needles, cast on **70 (74, 78, 86, 94)** sts using B and work 5cm in K2, P2 rib, starting and ending first row and every odd row (RS) with K2. Change to 6mm needles, cont in Fair Isle patt and dec 2 (0, inc 2, 0, dec 2) sts evenly, starting with 1 edge st and first st of chart 1.
68 (74, 80, 86, 92) sts.
Once the 13 rows of chart are completed, cont in st st using M and inc **2 (0, dec 2, 0, inc 2)** sts evenly on first row.
70 (74, 78, 86, 94) sts.
When work measures 30cm from end of ribbing, shape raglan by dec **2 (1, 2, 2, 2)** sts at each end, then cast off at beg of each row as follows: 1 st 10 times (1 st 12 times; 1 st 14 times; *1 st 4 times, 2 sts twice*, rep from * to * twice in total and finish with 1 st 4 times; *1 st twice, 2 sts twice*, rep from * to * 4 times in total and finish with 2 sts twice).
When work measures **35 (36, 37, 38, 39)** cm from end of ribbing, leave rem **56 (60, 60, 62, 62)** sts on holder.

FRONT
With 5.5mm needles, cast on **70 (74, 78, 86, 94)** sts using B and work 5cm in K2, P2 rib, starting and ending first row and every odd row (RS) with K2. Change to 6mm needles, cont in Fair Isle patt and dec **2 (0, inc 2, 0, dec 2)** sts evenly, starting with 1 edge st and first st of chart 1.
68 (74, 80, 86, 92) sts.
Once the 13 rows of the chart are completed, cont in st st using M and inc **2 (0, dec 2, 0, inc 2)** sts evenly on first row.
70 (74, 78, 86, 94) sts.
When work measures 30cm from end of ribbing, shape raglan by dec **2 (1, 2, 2, 2)** sts at each end, then cast off at beg of each row as follows: 1 st 4 times (1 st 6 times; 1 st 8 times; 1 st 4 times, 2 sts twice and 1 st 4 times; *1 st twice, 2 sts twice* rep from * to * 3 times in total).
When work measures **32.5 (33.5, 34.5, 35.5, 36.5)** cm from end of ribbing, leave rem **62 (66, 66, 70, 72)** sts on holder.

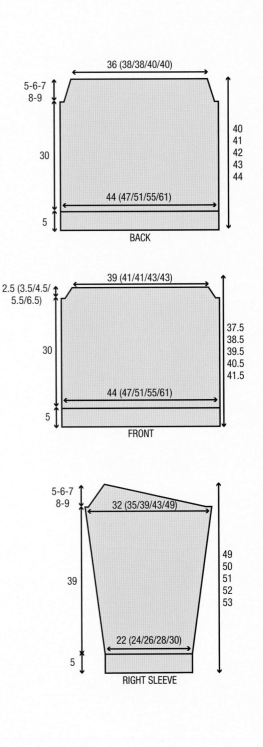

BACK

36 (38/38/40/40)

5-6-7 8-9

30

40 41 42 43 44

44 (47/51/55/61)

5

FRONT

39 (41/41/43/43)

2.5 (3.5/4.5/ 5.5/6.5)

30

37.5 38.5 39.5 40.5 41.5

44 (47/51/55/61)

5

RIGHT SLEEVE

5-6-7 8-9

32 (35/39/43/49)

39

49 50 51 52 53

22 (24/26/28/30)

5

RIGHT SLEEVE

With 5.5mm needles, cast on **34 (38, 42, 42, 46)** sts using B and work 5cm in K2, P2 rib, starting and ending first row and every odd row (RS) with K2.

Change to 6mm needles and cont in Fair Isle patt, starting with 2nd st (1 edge st and first st; first st; first st; 3rd st) of chart 1.

Once the 13 rows of chart are completed, cont in st st using M.

At the same time, inc 1 each end of row as follows: every 10th row 8 times (every 10th row 8 times; every 10th row 5 times and every 8th row 4 times; every 8th row 6 times and every 6th row 6 times; every 6th row 13 times and every 4th row twice).

50 (54, 60, 66, 76) sts.

When work measures 39cm from end of ribbing, shape raglan by dec **2 (1, 2, 2, 2)** sts at each end, then cast off at beg of each row as follows: 1 st 4 times (1 st 6 times; 1 st 8 times; 1 st 4 times, 2 sts twice and 1 st 4 times; *1 st twice, 2 sts twice* rep from * to * 3 times in tot).

When work measures **41.5 (42.5, 43.5, 44.5, 45.5)** cm from end of ribbing, leave RH sts on holder every alt row as follows: 13 sts 3 times (14 sts twice and 15 sts once; 15 sts 3 times; 15 sts twice and 16 sts once; 16 sts once and 17 sts twice).

At the same time, cast off at LH edge as follows: 1 st once then 1 st every alt row twice (1 st once then 1 st every alt row twice; 1 st once then 1 st every alt row twice; 2 sts once then 1 st every alt row twice; 1 st once then 2 sts every alt row once and 1 st on foll alt row once).

Make left sleeve, reversing shaping.

Polo-neck sweater cont'd

YOKE COLLAR

Start in middle of back with 6mm circular needle and take back from holder
28 (30, 30, 31, 31) sts from back, the **39 (43, 45, 46, 50)** sts from left sleeve,
knitting tog the last st of back with first st of left sleeve, then the **62 (66, 66,
70, 72)** sts from front, knitting tog the last st from left sleeve with first st from
front, then the **39 (43, 45, 46, 50)** sts of right sleeve, knitting tog the last st
of front with first st of right sleeve, and finally the rem **28 (30, 30, 31, 31)** sts
from back, knitting tog the last st from right sleeve with first of sts from back.
192 (208, 212, 220, 230) sts.
Work 2 rows of st st using M and dec **2 (8, 2, 0, 0)** sts evenly on first row (i.e.
dec 1 on back and 1 on front (dec 3 on back and front and dec 1 on each
sleeve; i.e. dec 1 on back and 1 on front; 0; 0).
190 (200, 210, 220, 230) sts remain.
Cont to follow yoke chart.
On 17th row of chart, **114 (120, 126, 132, 138)** sts remain.
Dec **18 (24, 30, 32, 38)** sts evenly on 29th row, i.e. dec **6 (7, 9, 9, 10)** sts on
back and front and dec **3 (5, 6, 7, 9)** sts on sleeves.
96 (96, 96, 100, 100) sts remain.
Once the 29 rows of chart are completed, work 4 rows of st st using M then
change to pair of 5.5mm needles and work 8cm in K2, P2 rib, using M and
starting first row with K2, then cast off loosely in rib.

TO MAKE UP AND FINISH

Join raglan and side seams.
Join sleeve seams.
Make **19 (20, 21, 22, 23)** bobbles as follows: With 5.5mm needles, cast on 2
sts using A. Work 3 times into first st and drop the second stitch. Turn and P3,
turn and K3, turn and P3, turn and SL1 onto RHN, K2tog, PSSO and fasten off.
Attach a bobble beneath each of the A-coloured tips below the yoke.

YOKE CHART

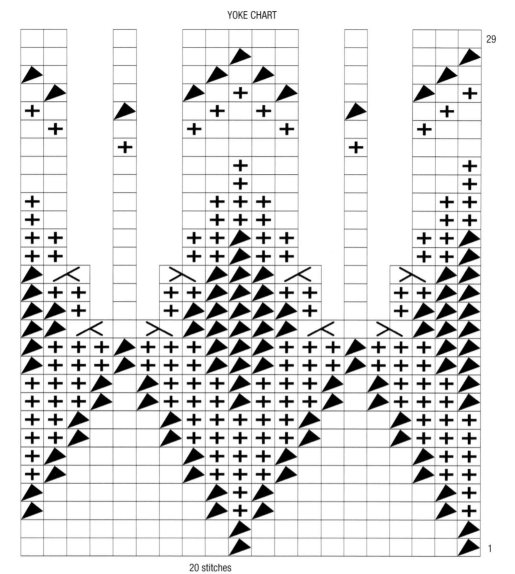

29

20 stitches

1

Repeat the 20 sts of chart

▶ 1st contrast colour (A)
+ 2nd contrast colour (B)
　 Main colour (M)
╱╲ K2tog using (B)
╲╱ SL1,K1, PSSO using (B)

Acknowledgements

We would like to thank:

Design Location
www.designlocation.fr

Nationale 7
nationale7paris.com

The '50s

Thank you to our models, Dovile, Marie, Megghann and Guillaume.

Sisley shirt, Paul Smith tie, Paul & Joe glasses, Sisley belt, Izac trousers, Minelli shoes

Antoine & Lili skirt, Wing bracelet, Tara Jarmon shoes

Gap jeans, Maison Boinet belt, Paul Smith shoes

Cos skirt, Fried bracelet, Guess clutch bag, Michel Vivien pumps

CK Jeans, Lolita Lempicka glasses, Max Kibardin shoes

Tara Jarmon skirt, Louis Pion watch, Lancaster bag, Paul Smith shoes

Tara Jarmon skirt and shoes, Louis Pion watch

Cherry Chau hat, Caroll trousers, Maison Boinet belt, Max Kibardin shoes

The '60s

IKKS shirt, Esprit jeans, Minelli shoes

Agnès b. shirt and trousers, Paul Smith tie, Minelli shoes

Bel Air skirt, Repetto shoes

Mango skirt, Thierry Lasery glasses, Repetto shoes

Caroll skirt, Paul Smith boots

La Bagagerie belt, Dim tights, Swildens glasses

Fabio tights, Scooter bracelets

Tosca Blu bag, Dim tights, Poggi ring, Repetto shoes

Dim tights, Repetto shoes

JB Martin boots, Dim tights

The '70s

Gap jeans, Gartane boots

Acquaverde trousers, Fried bracelets, Free Lance boots

Madeleine wide-brimmed hat, André sandals, Mes Demoiselles skirt

Vintage Lee trousers, Poggi rings, Castaner boots

Pascale Monvoisin ring, Paul & Joe ankle boots

Pomandère blouse, Caroll trousers, André sandals

Agatha earrings, Chattawak trousers, Castaner boots

IKKS shirt, Vintage Levis trousers, Esprit belt, Sisley shoes

Sisley shirt and shoes, Vintage Lee trousers, Esprit belt

Conversion Charts

While it is possible to use alternative yarns to those stated in the pattern, care should be taken in achieving the correct tension.
We cannot accept responsibility for the finished product if any yarn other than the specified yarn is used.

Yarn Details

Needle size	Tension: sts x rows	Phildar yarn	Metres per ball	Knit as:
7mm	11 x 16	RAPIDO	41	Chunky
	12 x 17	NEBULEUSE	51	Chunky
	12 x 17	TERRE NEUVE	42	Chunky
6mm	11 x 18	NEIGE	60	Chunky
	15 x 21	PARTNER 6	66	Chunky
	15 x 21	FRIMAS	79	Aran weight
	17 x 20	PHIL LIGHT	287	3-ply
5mm	17 x 23	BEAUGENCY	86	Aran weight
	16 x 22	PHIL HARMONY	69	Aran weight
4mm	18 x 28	PHIL OURSON	97	Aran weight
	19 x 26	LAINE MOHAIR & SOIE	96	Aran weight
	19 x 27	ILIADE	84	Aran weight
	19 x 27	QUIÉTUDE	90	Aran weight
3.5mm	22 x 31	ZEPHYR	139	DK
	22 x 29	LAINE COTON	95	DK
	23 x 30	PARTNER 3.5	111	Sport weight, 5-ply
	24 x 31	PUR ANGORA	109	4-ply
2.5 - 3mm	30 x 39	SUNSET	200	4-ply

UK, USA Yarn Equivalents

UK	USA
3-ply	Sock or light fingering
4-ply 5-ply, Sport weight, Lightweight DK	Fingering or Sport Sport
Double Knitting	8-ply, Light worsted
Aran weight	10-ply, Worsted, Fisherman, Medium weight
Chunky	12-ply, Bulky

Terminology

UK	USA
Tension	Gauge
Cast off	Bind off
Stocking stitch	Stockinette stitch
Yarn round needle	Yarn over
Double crochet	Single crochet
Triple crochet	Double crochet

Needle Sizes

Metric	Old UK	USA
2mm	14	0
2.25mm	13	1
2.5mm		
2.75mm	12	2
3mm	11	
3.25mm	10	3
3.5mm		4
3.75mm	9	5
4mm	8	6
4.5mm	7	7
5mm	6	8
5.5mm	5	9
6mm	4	10
6.5mm	3	$10^{1}{}_{,2}$
7mm	2	
7.5mm	1	
8mm	0	11
9mm	00	13
10mm	000	15

Abbreviations

K	=	knit
P	=	purl
st(s)	=	stitch(es)
cm	=	centimetres
mm	=	millimetres
RS	=	right side of work
WS	=	wrong side of work
st st	=	stocking stitch: K on RS, P on WS
rev st st	=	reverse stocking stitch: P on RS, K on WS
rep	=	repeat/repeating
cont	=	continue/continuing
alt	=	alternate
patt	=	pattern
dec	=	decrease/ decreasing
inc	=	increase/increasing
foll	=	following
rem	=	remaining
beg	=	beginning
tog	=	together
yrn	=	yarn round needle
yo	=	yarn over
Sl	=	slip next stitch
PSSO	=	pass slipped stitch over
tot	=	total
sep	=	separately
K2tog	=	knit 2 together
RH	=	right hand
LH	=	left hand
RHN	=	right hand needle
LHN	=	left hand needle
CN	=	cable needle
DK	=	double knitting
M1k	=	Make 1 st by picking up horizontal loop between sts
dbl	=	double
sgl	=	single
ch	=	chain
dc	=	double crochet (US single crochet)
tr	=	triple crochet (US double crochet)
yrh	=	yarn round hook
ch st	=	chain stitch
edge st	=	edge stitch (selvedge stitch)
( )	=	brackets refer to larger sizes

Sizing Charts

Womenswear

European Sizing	34-36	38-40	42-44	46-48	50-52
UK Sizing	6-8	10-12	14-16	18-20	22-24
US Sizing	2-4	6-8	10-12	14-16	18-20

Menswear

European Sizing	15-17 years	42-44	46-48	50-52	54-56
UK/US Sizing	S	M	L	XL	XXL
Chest Size (cm)	-	84-88	92-96	100-104	108-112

A DAVID & CHARLES BOOK
© Editions Marie Claire, Ltd 2013
Originally published as Tricoter Vintage

First published in the UK and USA in 2014 by F&W Media International, Ltd
David & Charles is an imprint of F&W Media International, Ltd
Brunel House, Forde Close, Newton Abbot, TQ12 4PU, UK

F&W Media International, Ltd is a subsidiary of F+W Media, Inc
10151 Carver Road, Suite #200, Blue Ash, OH 45242, USA

A catalogue record for this book is available from the British Library.

ISBN-13: 978-1-4463-0517-1 paperback
ISBN-10: 1-4463-0517-1 paperback

Printed in China by RR Donnelley for:
F&W Media International, Ltd
Brunel House, Forde Close, Newton Abbot, TQ12 4PU, UK

10 9 8 7 6 5 4 3 2
Editor: Thierry Lamarre
Aquisitions Editor (UK): Ame Verso
Desk Editor (UK): Charlotte Andrew
Design & Development: Charlotte Rion
Designers (UK): Anna Fazakerley & Jennifer Stanley
Photography: Pierre Nicou
Styling: Laurence Alexandre
Created by: Christelle Ledoux for Phildar
Digital retouching: Jean Michel Boillot
Instructions, charts, grids, knitting and diagrams: Yolaine Fournie
Graphic design & page layout: Either Studio
Cover: Either Studio
Proofreading, revision: Véronique Blanc
Pattern checker (UK): Caroline Voaden
Phildar Coordination Manager: Myriam Prez
Senior Production Controller (UK): Kelly Smith

F+W Media publishes high quality books on a wide range of subjects.
For more great book ideas visit: www.stitchcraftcreate.co.uk